THE GREAT
HISPANIC HERITAGE

Diego Rivera

Second Edition

THE GREAT HISPANIC HERITAGE

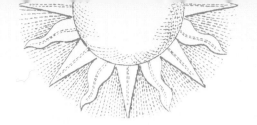

THE GREAT HISPANIC HERITAGE

Diego Rivera,
Second Edition

Sheila Wood Foard and Jamie Pietras

CHELSEA HOUSE
PUBLISHERS
An imprint of Infobase Publishing

Chelsea House
An imprint of Infobase Publishing
132 West 31st Street
New York NY 10001

Library of Congress Cataloging-in-Publication Data
Pietras, Jamie.
  Diego Rivera / Jamie Pietras. — 2nd ed.
     p. cm. — (Great Hispanic heritage)
  Rev. ed. of: Diego Rivera / Sheila Wood Foard. 2003.
  Includes bibliographical references and index.
  ISBN 978-1-60413-845-0 (hardcover)
  1. Rivera, Diego, 1886–1957—Juvenile literature. 2. Artists—Mexico—Biography—Juvenile literature. I. Rivera, Diego, 1886–1957. II. Foard, Sheila Wood. Diego Rivera.
III. Title. IV. Series.
  N6559.R55F63 2011
  759.972—dc22
  [B]   2010009480

Chelsea House books are available at special discounts when purchased in bulk quantities for businesses, associations, institutions, or sales promotions. Please call our Special Sales Department in New York at (212) 967-8800 or (800) 322-8755.

You can find Chelsea House on the World Wide Web at http://www.chelseahouse.com

Text design by Terry Mallon
Cover design by Terry Mallon/Alicia Post
Composition by EJB Publishing Services
Cover printed by Bang Printing, Brainerd, MN
Book printed and bound by Bang Printing, Brainerd, MN
Date printed: September 2010
Printed in the United States of America

10 9 8 7 6 5 4 3 2 1

This book is printed on acid-free paper.

All links and Web addresses were checked and verified to be correct at the time of publication. Because of the dynamic nature of the Web, some addresses and links may have changed since publication and may no longer be valid.

Contents

Artist at the Crossroads

If Diego Rivera had been a professional athlete in 1932, people could have said he was "at the top of his game." This artist from Mexico, whom many called the most famous muralist (painter of art on walls) in the world, was in demand to paint frescoes (paintings on freshly spread moist plaster) on the walls of public buildings in his own country, as well as in the United States.

MURAL IN DETROIT

Rivera signed a contract that year to paint frescoes on several walls at the Detroit Institute of Arts showing the development of industry in Michigan. Edsel Ford, president of both the motorcar company and the art institute's board, agreed to pay the artist nearly $21,000 to do the work. This was a great deal of money at the peak of the Great Depression (1929 to about 1939). It arrived at a time when more than 300,000 workers in Detroit had been laid off by the automobile industry, and workers who still had jobs had seen their wages cut from $33 to $22 a week.

Controversy erupted over the Detroit frescoes even before Rivera completed them. In the minds of some citizens, the fact that Rivera was a Communist (member of a political group that doesn't believe in private ownership of capital) added to the insult of such a large fee being paid to a foreign artist. It did not seem to matter that four years earlier Rivera had been expelled from the Mexican Communist Party for disagreeing with the party line.

When Rivera did arrive in Detroit, it was not to paint Communist propaganda. It was to realize his life's dream. He said in his autobiography, "Years before [while studying art in Paris], . . . I had envisioned the mural as the art form of the industrial society of the future."

Indeed, his embrace of muralism set up Rivera as one of the leading artists in a movement that included fellow Mexican painters José Orozco and David Siqueiros. Though each differed both in their style and political beliefs, they were unified by their conviction that art could be deployed for the public good.

When Rivera arrived in Detroit, anti-Communist sentiment was beginning to take hold in dramatic ways. A March 7, 1932, hunger march organized by the Communist Party had ended in violence when Ford security officers and Dearborn police fired on marchers, killing four of them. If Rivera was an artist in the service of Communism, however, he wasn't getting any support where it may have been expected. Members of the Communist Party, who had previously denounced Rivera as a renegade, had increased their attacks on him after his recent one-man show at the Museum of Modern Art in New York proved to be a popular success, drawing the museum's biggest attendance numbers at the time.

Detroit, the largest, most technically advanced industrial center in the world, was the perfect place for Diego Rivera to paint his murals. Standing more than six feet tall and weighing about 300 pounds, Rivera was a mountain of a man. He looked at the world he painted out of dark, intelligent, bulging eyes, often described as froglike. Frida Kahlo, his third wife and an artist in her own right, speculated that his eyes enlarged "his field of vision beyond that of most persons . . . almost as if they were constructed exclusively for a painter of vast spaces and multitudes."

Rivera's hands, though small, were capable of controlling a paintbrush for hours in an unhurried, sure manner. He moved slowly, in a rather cumbersome fashion, but he had the stamina of a workingman, perhaps of several workingmen. Such stamina is required of the fresco artist, whose giant art requires him to sit for 8, 12, sometimes 16 hours on the sagging plank of a wooden scaffold (temporary platform for working above ground level), painstakingly painting a picture on a freshly plastered wall. *Fresco* is an Italian word meaning "fresh." Fresco painting involves brushing watercolors onto fresh, wet plaster. The artist races against time because the plaster gradually becomes too dry to absorb the pigment, and the artist must stop. Painting begins again only after assistants apply fresh plaster to a new section of the wall.

At midnight on July 25, 1932, Diego Rivera, dressed in overalls and shoes already splattered with paint and plaster, climbed the ladder of his scaffold in the enclosed, marble-floored Garden Court of the Detroit Institute of Arts. Taking up his palette and paintbrush, he began the first of 27 fresco panels.

Earlier in the day, his assistants, highly skilled painters and masons, had completed the preliminary work of plastering and then tracing and stenciling his sketches onto the wet plaster. Under artificial light, Rivera started with the monochrome (one-color) outlines of his designs. He worked through the night until sunlight shone through the courtyard's clear glass roof. Then he painted in color. As long as the plaster remained fresh, he painted night after night and day after day for eight months, despite temperatures that reached 120 degrees

During the Great Depression, the Ford Motor Company commissioned
Diego Rivera to create a mural depicting the development of the automobile industry. The mural, a detail from which is shown here, high-
lighted the movement and life of the industrial workplace.

Fahrenheit or high humidity that kept his elephantine body, his fine hair, his baggy clothes, and, of course, the plaster moist for hours.

During the painting of the panels in Detroit, the giant man, whose need for energy was at its greatest, followed a strict diet, prescribed by a well-meaning doctor. It consisted of little more than citrus fruits and raw vegetables. Rivera lost more than 100 pounds. His skin hung on him in sagging folds. He looked sick, even hideous. When his wife, Frida, returned from a trip to Mexico to deal with a family emergency, she did not recognize him at the train station. After he introduced himself, she cried. To console her, he explained that the weight loss had resulted in increased quickness of movement, which would mean he could finish the Detroit frescoes sooner than originally planned.

Frida returned to Mexico in October. Rivera's painting of the frescoes at the Detroit Institute of Arts continued until March 13, 1933. While he painted these monumental works, he remained absorbed by their industrial theme. Machines had fascinated Rivera all his life. His earliest drawings, done when he was a child, had been of mechanical toys and loco-motives. He believed machines were beautiful. They embodied the human spirit, the spirit of the men who had designed and built them. As an artist of the industrial age, he wanted to paint huge pictures of machines.

His Detroit frescoes are narrative art, the story of men and women making automobiles. Before Rivera the storyteller could tell this exciting story, however, he had to see it happen right before his eyes. So he spent three months watching cars being built. He toured the Ford and Chrysler plants as well as other related factories, machine shops, and scientific laborato-ries, and he sketched steelworkers, welders, drill press opera-tors, assembly line workers, and all the other specially trained laborers doing their jobs.

Rivera's two largest panels are 800 square feet each. On the north wall, he painted *Detroit Industry: Production and*

Manufacture of Engine and Transmission. It shows workers at various stages of the process—in a foundry, at conveyor belts, along an assembly line—building the interior of a car. He included the manufacture of the Ford Company's 1932 V-8 engine and transmission.

On the south wall, Rivera painted *Detroit Industry: Production of Automobile Exterior and Final Assembly*. This shows the skilled workers in the body shop operating the huge body-pressing machine and preparing the body to go onto the frame.

The smaller panels above, below, and on both sides of the main panels—along with more panels on the west and east walls—tell the rest of the complex story. The natural resources found in the region, aviation in times of war and peace, the races of man, and agricultural and scientific achievements appear in no particular order. Everywhere in this dramatic celebration of the making of a car there is movement and life.

UNVEILING THE MURAL

As soon as the frescoes were unveiled, 20,000 people a day—record crowds—visited the museum to have a look at Rivera's work. Rivera's recollection of those first days after he finished the paintings, however, focuses on the initial negative reaction to his art. Well-dressed society ladies complained that the Garden Court of the museum had once been an oasis of peace and beauty. Where plants and flowers had once been, there were paintings of noisy, smelly, dirty machines that spewed smoke and dripped oil. They asked why Rivera had not chosen a more pleasant subject to paint. He responded that factories were both important and beautiful. His answer did not please them.

The controversy over the murals now centered on one panel, titled *Vaccination*, which appeared above and to the right of the main panel on the north wall. Rivera wrote, "The panel was intended to celebrate the noble work of men of science fighting against disease." It shows an infant in the arms of a nurse. A doctor is vaccinating the child. In the foreground are a horse, a cow, and some sheep—animals from which many vaccines are derived. In the background are three scientists at work in a laboratory. This panel was widely misinterpreted. Because the infant's blond hair resembled a halo, many viewers said the panel portrayed a modern nativity scene, the Holy Family in the manager with the three Magi. They labeled it sacrilegious.

Critics demanded that all the murals be whitewashed or in some other way removed from the walls. In newspaper articles, radio shows, and public speeches (some even from pulpits), people who represented various political, religious, and civic groups claimed the art was "Communistic," "anti-American," "an insult to Detroit," "pornographic," and "an advertising gimmick thought up by Edsel Ford."

Other groups countered the criticism with praise for the frescoes. They were "monumental realism" and a "study of American mechanical genius," said a representative of the Detroit Institute of Arts. According to Rivera, a group of engineers who worked in Detroit's steel and automobile factories admired the paintings because they were technically correct. Rivera felt both elation and pride to hear such approval from the very men most qualified to evaluate the accuracy of his work. Finally, Edsel Ford, who had played a major role in commissioning the art, said simply that he liked the murals. That quieted the critics.

Diego Rivera's masterpiece celebrating modern industry was saved from destruction in an outpouring of public admiration. The great muralist had done things his way, and he had stayed true to his artistic vision. He was successful because public opinion was on his side. But his triumph was short-lived.

MURAL IN NEW YORK CITY

When Rivera moved on to New York City to paint his next important fresco, a painting to cover 1,071 square feet in the lobby of the new Radio Corporation Arts (RCA) building in Rockefeller Center, his controversial art met quite a different fate. Rivera found several things unsettling from the beginning of this ambitious project. He believed that the Rockefeller family, specifically Nelson Rockefeller, the 25-year-old son of John D. Rockefeller Jr., was commissioning the work. In reality, it was the board of the engineering firm that managed Rockefeller Center and the architect they employed who made the decisions. These men knew what kind of art they wanted, and Rivera's vision did not suit them. Rivera insisted on doing a fresco in color, instead of a painting on board in black, white, and gray. After some negotiating, the architect and managers reluctantly agreed, perhaps in part because the other two well-known artists they had approached to do the mural, Pablo Picasso and Henri Matisse, declined.

The fee of $21,000 to be paid Rivera seemed high, but the artist had to pay his own assistants, including the plasterers and artists who ground his colors, traced his sketches on the wall, stenciled them on the wet plaster, and painted the less important backgrounds. For this job he hired more helpers than usual to complete the work by the deadline Nelson Rockefeller proposed—May 1. This date was significant to Rivera, because it was a day of national celebration in Communist countries.

The theme of the fresco was not left up to Rivera as it had been in Detroit. Its wordy title was *Man at the Crossroads Looking with Hope and High Vision to the Choosing of a New and Better Future.* Lengthy instructions accompanied the title. Rivera replied with even lengthier written descriptions of the art he proposed. He also submitted a sketch.

After an agreement was finally reached, Rivera began to paint in March 1933. From the start, he did not hide the fact that he was painting a revolutionary mural, one that expressed his political view. He preferred socialism to capitalism, so he would portray socialism as a better choice than capitalism. The Rockefellers knew Rivera was a Communist, and they had approved his preliminary sketch, but the design changed as he painted.

World-renowned artist Diego Rivera changed his painting style several times before creating the politically charged murals that would bring him fame. Rivera was known for living a passionate life, most notably as a member of the Communist Party and as husband to fellow artist Frida Kahlo.

What went on the center of the wall was a worker at the controls of a machine. Two elongated ellipses crossed in front of him. Cells, bacteria, and tissues as seen through a microscope decorated one of these; comets, suns, solar systems as seen through a telescope decorated the other. On the left were scenes in a capitalist country—a nightclub, a battlefield, and a group of policemen controlling a demonstration of unemployed workers. On the right were scenes in a socialist country—women athletes at a stadium, May Day celebrations, and a Communist leader grasping the hands of an African-American and a Russian soldier, allies of the future. The Communist leader was Lenin, the deceased founder of the Soviet Union.

Rivera intended Lenin's role in the alliance to be symbolic. However, Nelson Rockefeller knew that having Lenin's face in the fresco would offend a great many Americans, as he told Rivera in a carefully worded letter asking the artist to replace Lenin's features with those of an unknown man.

Rivera would rather see the entire fresco destroyed than replace Lenin's features. In a politely written response, he supported his stand by stating that the original sketch, approved before the painting began, had included Lenin's portrait. This was not entirely true. Perhaps his knack for storytelling interfered with good judgment. The sketch had contained the scene in question, but the figure that was now Lenin had been a man whose face was partly covered by a cap.

Rivera suggested replacing the nightclub scene on the opposite side with a more positive image, such as Abraham Lincoln, who abolished slavery. The response to his suggestion came a few days later while the artist was working high on the scaffold. A group of men representing the Rockefellers arrived. One asked the artist to come down. After he did, the man gave him a check for the rest of the fee owed him ($14,000) and told him to stop work. Some of the men escorted the artist and his assistants out of the building, while others climbed the scaffold and covered the fresco with a large canvas screen.

News of the censorship (action of examining and then suppressing or deleting a controversial idea) spread quickly. It became a cause célèbre (incident that causes widespread attention), especially in the art world. The public wanted to see the mural. Demonstrators picketed outside the building. Artists from around the world and other concerned citizens sent messages of support.

Not all the voices spoke in favor of the art, however. Many people agreed with the actions taken. Rivera's next commission to decorate the General Motors Building at the Chicago World's Fair was immediately canceled.

Man at the Crossroads remained behind the screen, but Rockefeller representatives issued statements claiming that Rivera would be allowed to complete the work when he agreed to make changes. The reality, however, was that the managers and the architect in charge had not liked the fresco from the beginning. They did not want it on their wall.

In a newspaper article, the Rockefellers assured the public that the fresco would not be destroyed but would remain covered for an unspecified time. Discussions began concerning the careful—and costly—removal of the mural to the Museum of Modern Art, which was not far away.

Because Rivera had been paid in full, he could do little to change the impending outcome. He pledged to paint a reproduction of the art if a suitable wall were found. Several offers were made, but none of the walls seemed appropriate. Rivera stayed in the United States for a few more months, painting *Portrait of America*, an uninspired history of the United States on movable panels in a run-down school building in New York. When his money ran out (it dwindled quickly after he paid his agent and assistants), he returned to Mexico, angry, humiliated, and confused. In ill health, he fell into depression.

On Saturday, February 9, 1934, at midnight, workers entered the lobby of the RCA Building. Using axes, they demolished *Man at the Crossroads Looking With Hope to the Choosing of a New and Better Future*. The blows that reduced the fresco to fine bits of plaster also destroyed Diego Rivera's dreams of covering the walls of the United States with murals.

The great muralist had entered the United States at the "top of his game." He left in defeat. But defeat comes to all men and women, athletes and artists alike. Rivera acknowledged as much on the day when his Detroit frescoes were in danger of being destroyed. He wrote that in such an event he would be distressed. Yet on the following day, he would begin painting again "for I am not merely an 'artist' but a man performing his biological function of producing paintings, just as a tree produces flowers and fruit."

Back in Mexico, Diego Rivera prepared to paint again.

The Magnificent Painter

The birthplace of the *pintor magnífico* (magnificent painter) was a three-story stone house at 80 Pocitos Street in Guanajuato, an old silver-mining town in central Mexico. The year of Rivera's birth was 1886. But was the date December 8, the Feast of the Immaculate Conception, as his mother always claimed? Or was it December 13? A civil document found in the town hall records the first date; a baptismal certificate records the second.

Did Rivera's birth certificate give his name as José Diego Rivera or Diego María Rivera? Here again there is disagreement. The painter himself, a storyteller fond of embellishing the facts of his life, said he was christened Diego María de la Concepción Juan Nepomuceno Estanislao de Rivera y Barrientos Acosta y Rodríguez. Whether this long name was his mother's choice or the product of his own active imagination, it is certain that his parents were overjoyed when he was born alive. All three of his mother's earlier pregnancies had resulted in stillbirths. On those occasions, the disappointed father, Don Diego de Rivera, presented his wife with a large doll. He wished to console her as well as to show that he did not blame her for the losses.

Twenty-two-year-old María del Pilar Barrientos was a tiny, nervous woman with large, innocent eyes. She was a mestizo (part European and part Indian). Don Diego, a criollo (of European descent) and a tall, powerfully built, handsome man with a black beard, was 15 years older than his wife and nearly twice her size.

BIRTH OF THE TWINS

Diego was the first twin born on that December night and so was named after his father. His twin brother arrived a short time later. Named Carlos María Rivera (some say José Carlos Rivera), he died before he reached the age of two years.

A photograph of the boys at about 10 months reveals they were not identical twins. Diego's face is rounder and his straight hair is shorter. Fat legs portend the bulk that was to come. He slouches against the back of a small chair and holds his right hand to his mouth. He is sucking his thumb. During his second year, he would put that hand to better use, drawing his first pictures.

Both of young Diego's parents were educated. His mother had been homeschooled by private tutors, a rarity for a Mexican woman at that time. At age 18, she began teaching music and grammar in a primary school, which her mother, Doña Nemesia Rodríguez de Valpuesta, founded after she became a widow.

Diego's father, known to be a man of intelligence, entered the Colegio de la Purísima Concepción at the age of 15. Later he attended the University of Guanajuato. Don Diego was a jack-of-all-trades and master of none. He had served in one of the Mexican armies that drove the French out of the country. After that, he trained to be an industrial chemist, then worked as an assayer and prospector in an unprofitable silver mine his family owned. He wrote a textbook on Spanish grammar and articles for a weekly newspaper called *El Demócrata*. His

Perhaps inspired by her grief over losing several pregnancies and Diego's twin brother, Diego Rivera's mother studied obstetrics and became a midwife. Although she was a staunch Catholic, her husband was a radical liberal, which may have influenced young Diego's political beliefs.

political leanings tended toward the liberal, which was unusual, since Guanajuato was a conservative town. Despite that, Don Diego served on the town's city council. He was also a teacher at the secondary level in the school where he met and fell in love with Diego's mother.

María's grief was so extreme when Diego's twin died that her doctor prescribed a distraction to bring her out of depression. She attended the university to study obstetrics and then became a midwife. Meanwhile, Diego was cared for by his wet nurse, a Tarascan Indian named Antonia. Diego remembered her fondly in later years, writing, "Visually she was an artist's ideal of the classic Indian woman, and I have painted her many times from memory in her long red robe and blue shawl."

YOUNG DIEGO

Diego's health was poor, though not as poor as his twin's. He suffered from rickets, a disease resulting in skeletal deformities because of inadequate sunlight or vitamin D. Antonia took him to her mountain village to cure him. There he stayed for two years, healing his body and strengthening his imagination. His stories about that time center on Antonia's cures with herbs and rituals. He claimed she was a sort of witch doctor who knew magic. She allowed him to roam the forest, where wild animals, even dangerous ones, became his friends and playmates. Upon his return to his mother, Diego seemed changed. María described him as a little Indian because he spoke Tarascan, not Spanish, to the family's parrot.

Diego was a precocious child. He walked earlier than most children and talked in long sentences, arguing with his parents when they attempted to discipline him. He told tall tales, which his father encouraged, but which brought much wringing of hands to his pious mother, a devout Catholic. At four, he learned to read. He drew pictures on everything he could reach—paper, envelopes, pages in books, and walls. After finding it impossible to curb the boy's artistic efforts, his father set aside one room in the house where Diego could draw all he desired. Supplied with paper, pencils, crayons, chalk, and, best of all, a black canvas that rose high on the walls, the boy drew his first murals of animals, mechanical toys, soldiers, locomotives, cabooses, bridges, train wrecks, and battles—including injured or wounded bodies strewn about the landscape.

MOVE TO MEXICO CITY

Nestled in a hollow at the foot of rugged mountains, Guanajuato is a beautiful city. It was Diego's home until he was six years old, when his mother suddenly decided to move her family to Mexico City. Possibly fearing the negative reaction to her husband's editorials in *El Demócrata*, María packed up her personal belongings and those of her children (Diego's sister, also named María, was born when he was five) and sold the rest of the household items. With her two small children, she boarded the train for Mexico City. Diego must have found the trip exciting. He had long been fascinated by the trains that arrived daily at the station where he was allowed to play.

When his father returned from a business trip, the neighbors told him where his family had gone. He followed immediately. Perhaps he was concerned for his safety, too. His liberal views were not well received by Guanajuato's politicians, especially when he urged citizens to concern themselves with the living conditions of the poor. The poor themselves could not read, and his words did little to improve their situation. Not long after the move, the Riveras heard that the staff of *El Demócrata* had been arrested. Later, Don Diego modified his liberal views.

Mexico City seemed big to the Riveras. Left forever were the quaint cobblestone streets and gaslights of the small town. In the "City of Palaces" there were wide boulevards, electric streetcars, huge railway stations, massive buildings, even theaters. But the Riveras had little money, so their standard of living dropped when they moved. Diego's father worked at several jobs before he found a good one. His mother gave birth to another baby boy, who lived less than a week. Diego became ill with scarlet fever, then with typhoid. Disease was prevalent in the poorer sections of the city, where so many lived in squalor.

Not until his father found a job with the Department of Public Health and his mother started working as a midwife did the family move to a better neighborhood. They had been in Mexico City for three years by that time. Diego was eight, and he wanted to go to school. He enrolled in a Catholic school of his mother's choosing, the Colegio del Padre Antonio. Three months later he dropped out. The next year he attended the Colegio Católico Carpentier, but he disliked that school, too. Diego was spoiled. He quit school again.

Not until he entered the Liceo Católico Hispano-Mexicano did he find a school and a teacher he liked. Here, a priest, Father Servine, gave him food, books, tools, and instruction that suited him. Because of the father's tutoring, Diego moved quickly from the third grade to the sixth.

ART SCHOOL

At 10 years old, Diego was tall and hefty for his age. His father thought, maybe hoped, his son's destiny lay in a military or engineering career because of his drawings of armies and trains. Of course, he was too young to pursue either of these studies. Besides, Diego insisted on art school, although students usually did not enter such a school until age 16. Perhaps his size helped him not to stand out as being much younger than the other students when his mother enrolled him at the San Carlos Academy of Fine Arts. Surely his talent for and love of drawing counted for more. He went to elementary school during the day and attended art school at night. He followed this tiring schedule for two years. Then he received a scholarship to attend art school during the day. Required classes included math, physics, chemistry, and natural history. The art curriculum was traditional—quite rigid—and boring. This certainly was not the child's play of earlier years when he filled the walls of his "first studio" with drawings of locomotives and toy soldiers.

Despite Diego's bulk, he had a lot of energy. But as a student, he spent long hours indoors, tediously copying reproductions, engraved replicas, and plaster casts—in other words,

BEING HISPANIC

DIEGO MEETS ARTIST POSADA

The legendary engraver whom Diego called a great folk artist and the most important of his teachers didn't actually work at Rivera's school. Rather, José Guadalupe Posada owned a small engraving shop on a street near the art school. During his career, he did more than 15,000 engravings on metal plates, which he then printed on colored tissue paper along with the tales, news stories, ballads, prayers, and jokes written and performed by singers who traveled to marketplaces throughout Mexico. These wandering minstrels and the tissue paper sheets they sold for a centavo were popular with the millions of illiterates who could not afford a real newspaper, even if they could have read it.

Posada's etchings and engravings featured the varied aspects of Mexican life—newsworthy events, such as the arrival by train of the uniformed body of General Manuel González to Mexico City (published not long before Diego's mother moved the family to the city), street brawls, public executions, fires, and train wrecks. "Portraits" ranged from the bandit Zapata to Porfirio Díaz, the Mexican dictator in power at that time, who claimed a landslide vote after every rigged (deceptively fixed) election. Skeletons were a specialty of Posada's and were, no doubt, especially popular in early November during the Day of the Dead celebrations, the festive time when Mexicans remember their loved ones who have died.

Although there is no evidence that Diego became Posada's student (as he sometimes claimed), Diego wrote, "It was he who revealed to me the inherent beauty in the Mexican people, their struggle and aspirations."

doing art exercises. Had he been a music student, these assignments would have been the equivalent of practicing scales. Only after two years of "copying" were students allowed to draw live models.

Diego's own works from these early years, which were kept in the school's archives, include a copy of a rococo (elaborate style) plaster ornament in low relief, a Venus de Milo (standing on her head), and a bust of Homer with a beard.

Diego said later that he was not happy artistically. This time, however, he did not drop out of school. Instead, he worked hard, learning artistic techniques, earning high grades, and winning prizes for his art. His instructors found his work to their liking.

ART TEACHER SANTIAGO REBULL

During his years in art school (he left at 16, the age when most students entered), Rivera had three teachers, or masters, whose instruction he especially appreciated. Of the three masters Diego studied under at San Carlos, Santiago Rebull, one of the leading Mexican artists, was in his 70's when Diego took his classes. Rebull had taught at the art school for 50 years. As a young man, he studied art in Paris with the master, Jean-Auguste-Dominque Ingres, a much-admired, influential French painter. Rebull considered Ingres the greatest artist of the nineteenth century and encouraged his own students to learn all they could from examining the works of that master.

One day when Diego was barely a teen, Rebull embarrassed him by finding fault with his drawing of a live model. His classmates, about 50 older students, watched with typical mocking curiosity. They had already noticed this fat boy with the froglike features, who dressed in bright pink socks and short pants. When he pulled pins, string, and earthworms from his pockets, they thought of him as a child better suited to fishing in the polluted canal than attempting the assignments of a serious art student.

But the students' expressions changed after Rebull's criticism ended in an invitation for Diego to visit his studio on the following day. After the master left the room, the other students flocked around Diego to see his drawing. What could Rebull have seen in the fat boy's art? According to rumor, the master had kept his studio off-limits to students for 20 years. Their cursory look at Diego's drawing convinced them that the old master was senile. They saw nothing exceptional in Diego's effort and made fun of him. "But the next day," Diego later recalled, "the old man told me what he had discovered in my work was an interest in life and movement. Such an interest, he said, is the mark of a genuine artist. 'These objects we call paintings,' he went on, 'are attempts to transcribe to a plane surface essential movements of life. A picture should contain the possibility of perpetual motion.'"

Diego valued Rebull's instruction. It changed the way he looked at art. From then on, he was more aware "of the laws of proportion and harmony, within which movement proceeds, and which are to be discerned in the masterpieces of all ages."

ART TEACHER FELIX PARRA

Another art teacher at San Carlos who influenced Diego was Felix Parra. His dark paintings, which were conventional in every respect, were not what attracted Diego. It was Parra's passion for the pre-Conquest Indian art of Mexico. Before the Spaniards came, the art of the Indians had been "related to the soil, the landscape, the forms, animals, deities, and colors of their own world. Above all, it had been emotion-centered."

After the Spanish Conquest (pursuit to conquer America and Mexico by the Spanish in the sixteenth century), Mexican artists imitated classical European art. Within the otherwise traditional curriculum at the school, a teacher who instilled in this particular student an appreciation for Aztec art must have been unusual indeed. (Aztecs were Nahuatl-speaking people who founded the Mexican empire in the sixteenth century.) Diego's resulting passion for pre-Conquest art stayed with him

At the San Carlos Academy, Rivera learned technique and imitated the masters. *The Threshing Floor* (1904) shows a typical Mexican landscape, clearly influenced by his teacher, the landscape artist José María Velasco.

for the rest of his life, coming to the forefront especially during the years he lived in his native Mexico.

ART TEACHER JOSÉ MARÍA VELASCO

The most famous of the masters Diego revered at San Carlos was José María Velasco, an excellent painter of portraits, but more often noted for his Mexican landscapes. Diego said he learned the laws of perspective from him. This master gave him much practical advice about technique. Studying under Velasco gave the young artist a chance to get outdoors. After years of working in a school, mostly under artificial light, Diego welcomed the chance to paint in the clear, bright, high-altitude light of Mexico City and the surrounding area. The snow-capped twin volcanoes, Iztaccíhuatl and Popocatépetl, made especially fine subjects.

After Diego left the art academy at the age of 16, he traveled the countryside for four years, painting the Mexican land, its people, and its villages. He practiced the techniques he learned from Velasco and the other masters. But the more canvases he covered (there were a great many at every stage of his career), the more dissatisfied he grew with his art. Even though his paintings were beginning to sell and others admired his work, Diego knew he must continue his study.

TRAVELS TO EUROPE

Diego wanted to go to Europe. But where would he get the money for such an adventure, the dream of nearly every serious aspiring artist? His father suggested the solution. Together, father and son traveled to the state of Veracruz to see the governor, a contact Don Diego made while working for the health department. They took along Diego's portfolio. After seeing evidence of young Diego's talent, the governor granted the youth a small monthly scholarship to be used for studying art in Europe. All that remained was for Diego to raise the funds needed for travel expenses. A showing—and the subsequent sales—of 12 of his oils and pastels, mainly landscapes, brought enough to pay for passage on the steamship *Alfonso XIII*.

Weighing in at slightly over 300 pounds and standing six feet tall, Diego Rivera was finished with child's play. He would study art in Spain. He was 20, and as he admitted later, "a dimwit . . . so vain, so full of the blackheads of youth and dreams of being master of the universe, just like all the other fools of the age."

3

Rivera
in Europe

Diego Rivera, the aspiring artist, arrived in Spain on a foggy
January day in 1907 ready to continue his art studies. Although
he had shaved his beard shortly before his departure from
Mexico, in photos taken around that time he had a disheveled,
unkempt look because of the baggy, wrinkled clothes covering
his great bulk.

ART STUDIES WITH CHICHARRO

Rivera traveled to Madrid, carrying with him a letter of
introduction from Gerardo Murillo (Dr. Atl), an influential
Mexican painter Rivera had known at San Carlos. Dr. Atl himself had studied briefly in Spain and wrote the letter to a youth-
ful, but traditional, Spanish painter named Eduardo Chicharro
y Aguera. Chicharro was to be Rivera's teacher. Diego found
Chicharro's studio, set up his easel, and started to paint. Day
after day, he painted from dawn until after midnight.

A self-portrait he did during his first year in Spain shows a bearded man in a dark suit and black hat, smoking a pipe. At a table, he sits alone, brooding over a half-empty bottle of beer. There is a romantic, yet somber, air about the portrait.

In addition to studio work, Chicharro took Rivera and his other students on tours across Spain to paint landscapes. Three of these that Rivera painted depict men at work; the others include no workers, no figures at all. Rivera also visited galleries and museums to see and copy the original works of important artists, including El Greco, Velázquez, and Goya. Always the storyteller, Rivera later claimed that he was very good at making copies, so good, in fact, that three of his paintings were shown as original Goyas and an El Greco in the United States and France. However, he would never reveal which "forgeries" were his.

Since he was in Europe on a scholarship granted by Don Teodora A. Dehesa, the governor of Veracruz, Rivera had to work hard to prove himself. This meant periodically sending paintings back to the governor. One, titled *Night in Avila*, is a lovely street scene. Another shows a church and rhododendrons in bloom. Rivera sent many picturesque landscapes like these and several portraits, but he did not send his self-portrait, perhaps feeling that its romantic mood would be an embarrassment. Also, Chicharro verified his pupil's exceptional talent and remarkable progress in writing to the governor.

The paintings pleased the governor, and the scholarship money of 300 francs a month continued. But the artist lamented later that his art from the two years he studied under Chicharro was flat. He wrote that he did little painting of any worth during his year and a half in Spain. His work from that time lacks originality, but it reveals he was mastering technique.

FIRST ART EXHIBIT

Rivera's first exhibit in Madrid came before he had been in the country one year. One critic noticed his work and predicted that he would become a great painter. But Rivera's life was quiet and dull during his stay in that city. Years later he "improved on" the facts. He especially liked to tell how he came up with enough money to leave Madrid. It began when an important visitor came to Chicharro's studio. He was Don Joaquín Sorolla y Bastida, a successful artist and master of technique. Sorolla asked to see work done by younger artists. Though there were many paintings on the walls, one of Rivera's, of course, caught his eye. It was called *The Blacksmith Shop*. He asked who had painted it. Chicharro told him the Mexican had. At this point in the story, Rivera explains, "'The Mexican' was my Madrid nickname, given to me because of the large sombrero I always wore, my head being so large that no ordinary-size Spanish hat would ever fit me." Perhaps Rivera's head was big in more ways than one.

Sorollo then took Rivera's right hand, looked at each of the young artist's fingers, and asked if he knew what he had in that hand. When Rivera answered no, Sorolla laughed and said, "In this finger you have a checkbook of American dollars, here a checkbook for pounds sterling, here a checkbook for Spanish pesetas, here a checkbook for Argentine pesos, and here a checkbook for French francs. . . . I guarantee you . . . if you paint day and night, you'll have twice as much money as I have . . . because [Chicharro] has told me you're an exceptionally hard worker."

Rivera concludes the story by saying that the next day, full of confidence because of Sorolla's compliment, he gambled in a local casino and won 3,500 pesetas, which he used to finance a tour of Europe. Rivera's confidence, however, did not last long.

PARIS

In the spring of 1909, Rivera arrived in Paris. Once there, he followed in the art student tradition of "copying at the Louvre, painting on the banks of the Seine, viewing exhibitions and attending the free schools of Montparnasse." But Rivera wrote later, "I was slow and timid in translating my inner feeling on canvas. I worked at my paintings in an indifferent, even listless way, lacking the confidence to express myself directly. My work of the period from 1909 through the first half of 1910 . . . still looks academic and empty."

Admitting that he was in awe of Paris, and of Europe in general—its history and culture, its masters like Michelangelo, Cézanne, Renoir—Rivera attributed his inability to develop an original style to what he labeled his "Mexican-American inferiority complex." He stayed in Paris about two months, then continued his European tour, traveling with Enrique Friedmann, another Mexican painter, to Brussels.

EUROPEAN TOUR

On a detour into the Flemish city of Bruges, he met and fell in love with Angeline Beloff, a pretty, blond-haired, blue-eyed Russian artist, who was seven years older than he was. Her traveling companion was the artist María Blanchard, whom Rivera had met at Chicharro's studio. Though Angeline would later return his love, his first declarations of love made her feel pressured and confused. Ultimately Angeline agreed to become his fiancée.

Together with two other artists, Angeline and Diego traveled to London, where they stayed a month, painting and visiting museums to study the art of such masters as Turner, Hogarth, and Blake. At the British Museum, an exhibit of pre-Columbian art made Rivera homesick for Mexico. And he was profoundly affected by the sight of the poor people of London, homeless children and adults eating garbage out of trashcans.

On their return to France, all four artists took up residence in Paris, renting separate studios. Rivera worked under a master named Victor-Octave Guillonet. His art remained academic; he perfected his technique. One landscape showed the effects of the London tour. This work, first titled *Le Port de la Tournelle*, later *Notre-Dame de Paris Through the Mist*, depicts three dockworkers unloading barrels of wine from a barge in the gray mist along the Seine. He also did his first portrait of Angeline, whom he would paint many times. But he still had not found a style he could call his own.

Rivera enjoyed a long relationship with Russian painter Angeline Beloff, and he painted many portraits of her, including this 1918 oil on canvas. The two lived together in Paris while Rivera continued to seek an artistic style that suited him. Together Rivera and Beloff had a son, Diego, who died at the age of 14 months.

RETURN TO MEXICO

In the summer of 1910, Rivera's homesickness for Mexico reached a peak. He felt restless, dissatisfied, and impatient. He would go home to exhibit his art at the San Carlos School of Fine Arts, where he had studied as a child. The governor of Veracruz gave him permission to return for the national centennial celebrations of Mexican independence that would also honor the dictator Porfirio Díaz, who had been in power for 30 years. The dictator was throwing an expensive party for himself.

Traveling through Madrid to pick up some of his canvases from storage, Rivera again saw several of El Greco's masterpieces. In a letter to Angeline, he described his emotional reaction to the Christian art of the master, whom he called a sublime painter, the greatest of the great painters. As he gazed at the *Pentecost, the Descent of the Holy Spirit,* he felt a spirit descend and fill him with beautiful feelings. For the first time, he said he understood the soul of that and El Greco's other paintings, and he attributed this understanding to having met and fallen in love with Angeline.

Rivera had not made his mark in Europe, but back in Mexico, he was an important upcoming artist. The canvases he sent to the governor of Veracruz had been widely shown and admired. Not only did his family meet him at the train station in Mexico City, but so did the press. A picture of the bearded young man wearing a suit and tie ran in the newspaper.

The national centennial celebrations—to cost 20 million pesos—were already under way. Thousands of people arrived in the capital to attend balls, watch parades, and go to carnivals. Many of these also saw the exhibition of Rivera's work, which opened on November 20, the same day that Francisco I. Madero began the Mexican Revolution against the Díaz regime.

The most important visitor at Diego's show was the wife of Díaz, Doña Carmen Romero Rubio de Díaz, who was sent in her husband's place while the dictator dealt with the troubles at hand. She bought several paintings. A number of others sold, too (some to San Carlos). When the show closed, Rivera had earned 4,000 pesos, the most he had been paid. The press described him as a great artist.

On the surface, everything went well. But 1910 proved to be a turning point in the history of Mexico. Later, Rivera would claim he had taken part in the rebellion against Díaz, also that he had planned to assassinate Díaz, but his plans went awry when Díaz sent his wife to the opening. Researchers doubt these claims. Rivera had grown up during the period known as the Porfiriato (the pre-revolutionary society ruled over by Porfirio Díaz), and the governor who supported Díaz financed Rivera's art studies in Europe.

MEXICAN REVOLUTION

There had been political unrest in Mexico for years, but Díaz had suppressed the opposition. In 1910, however, things were different. Despite having his opposing candidate, Francisco I. Madero arrested and thrown into prison, Díaz was unable to stop the liberal democrat Madero when he escaped and was joined by the soldiers dispatched to stop the revolution.

Eighty-year-old Díaz resigned from office in May 1911, rather than face the violence of being overthrown. He went into exile in Europe. For the next 10 years, a bloody, complicated civil war raged in Mexico. More than one million people died. Alvaro Obregón, a general who fought in the revolution, was elected in 1920. His term was short, but it marked the final end of the Díaz era.

The political climate of Mexico was changing in 1911 when Rivera exhibited the art he had painted in Europe. But he had been out of the country for four years and was out of touch with what was happening. The political unrest that was to have a profound effect on him later did little to change his life at that time except to provide some of the details for his tall tales.

RETURN TO PARIS

Not long after his successful show, Rivera took the money he earned from the sale of his paintings and returned to Paris (with a stop along the way to paint landscapes in the bright light of Mexico and then visit the galleries in Madrid). He went back to Angeline and his private quest to develop a distinctive style.

Rivera and Angeline were never legally married (at least no record has been located). He wrote: "For the next ten years that I spent in Europe, Angeline lived with me as my common-law wife. During all that time, she gave me

ADOLFO BEST MAUGARD

Diego Rivera counted the painter and filmmaker Adolfo Best Maugard among his friends. And though Best Maugard may never have achieved Rivera's level of fame, he does hold a special place in Mexican art history. Having worked tirelessly to create illustrations of pre-Columbian artifacts dug up from the Valley of Mexico early in his career, Best Maugard concluded that there were seven basic elements in their design, ultimately rooted in nature: the point and straight line, spiral, circle, semicircle or arc, wavy line, "s" shape, and zigzag. He eventually incorporated his findings in a book, and soon his teachings became part of Mexican school curriculum, to some controversy.

Rivera met Best Maugard in Europe in 1912, and the two found they had a lot to discuss about topics including Modernist painting, the need for art education, and a national artistic identity in Mexico. It was Best Maugard's influence that may have helped inspire Rivera to create work rooted in Mexican nationalism.

everything a good woman can give to a man. In return, she received from me all the heartache and misery that a man can inflict upon a woman." The couple rented an apartment in the free republic of Montparnasse, which had become a popular area for the many artists from around the world who crowded into Paris to study. Few of these artists had a lot of money, but some went on to fame and fortune. Rivera and Angeline were happy.

Rivera continued to paint in a traditional style. He was still mainly living off the scholarship from Mexico and had to please his sponsors. But when the couple spent the summer of 1912 in Spain (she made etchings of street scenes), he produced work that showed, for the first time, a distinctive, personal style. Artistically speaking, he was growing, breaking new ground.

After experimenting with various styles of the masters he admired, Rivera painted several canvases worthy of note, especially *Los Viejos* (The Old Ones), using elongated figures like those of El Greco. Against the dry, barren landscape of Spain are three old men whose facial expressions reveal their unique personalities. The colors are brighter than the palette he had been using, and there is movement, which he believed was vital in art. The painting is large, nearly seven feet by six feet, a size that foreshadows some of his later gigantic works. It was a beginning.

In September, the couple moved into an apartment on the top floor of a dilapidated building in Montparnasse, where they would stay for six years. Rivera got to know the artists, models, and hustlers who frequented the neighborhood's cafes, and he earned a reputation for his fantastic stories. He spun tales of fighting alongside Mexican revolutionary leader Emiliano Zapata and feasting on human flesh.

Back home, the view from his apartment window would not have suited an artist desiring a quiet spot in which to paint, but Rivera found the industrial scene attractive. Outside was the commotion of a rail yard, complete with smoke and noise day and night. No doubt it reminded him of his visits to the train station in Guanajuato as a child. Rivera's excitement on viewing the activity is evident in the excellent portrait he did of Adolfo Best Maugard, a Mexican friend whose enthusiasm for the folk art of their native land would have a permanent effect on Rivera.

In the elongated style of El Greco, Rivera portrayed the man elegantly dressed in a long, black, fur-trimmed coat; shiny, black shoes; and fine leather gloves. He is standing on a red footbridge that crosses over the railroad tracks. Behind him are a giant Ferris wheel and a cluster of industrial buildings shrouded in the smoke billowing from a moving locomotive. Rivera considered this the most important painting he had done up to that time, although it received less attention than he expected at its first showing.

CUBISM AND RIVERA

The *Portrait of Adolfo Best Maugard* was overshadowed by paintings done in the new style called cubism, a movement that caught Rivera's attention. Rivera had known of cubism before that show (it started around 1906), but he had not yet met the Spaniard, Pablo Picasso, who, along with Georges

In 1913, Rivera decided to become a cubist painter, a shift in styles that allowed him greater personal expression. It was during the painting of this portrait of Japanese artists Tsuguharu Foujita and Riichiro Kawashima that Rivera received word that the celebrated cubist painter Pablo Picasso wanted to meet him.

Braque, was the first of the cubist painters. Semiabstract and geometrical, these radically different paintings broke all the traditional rules of perspective by depicting several viewpoints of a subject at once.

In the summer of 1913, Rivera became a cubist painter. Perhaps it was because he needed money to support himself and Angeline. Madero had been assassinated in Mexico, where the revolution still raged, and Rivera's scholarship abruptly ended.

The cubists were not only getting attention from the critics; their works were selling. But Rivera also found the movement intriguing. Years later, he reflected: . . . [cubism] was a revolutionary movement, questioning everything that had previously been said and done in art. It held nothing sacred. As the old world would soon blow itself apart, never to be the same again, so cubism broke down forms as they had been seen for centuries, and was creating out of the fragments new forms, new objects, new patterns and—ultimately—new worlds.

During the next four years, with World War I raging in Europe, Diego Rivera painted nothing except cubist paintings. Perhaps he thought he had found his unique style.

Revolutionary Muralist

Diego Rivera's decision to become a cubist painter in 1913 resulted in his being noticed and praised immediately. The art press reported his switch in styles. His fame spread. His work sold. He supported himself with his art. During the next four years, he produced more than 200 cubist paintings.

As usual, he worked hard, but now Rivera was painting what he liked. Not content to copy other artists, who were working in the new style, he experimented. New York journalist Pete Hamill writes that, "Many of his Cubist paintings are superb: inventive, vigorous, surprising. Almost from the beginning, they were full of color; not for him the somber repression of color that characterized some who made line, form, and faceting the only permissible syntax of Cubism."

With the notice Rivera received came an important friendship. The artist he considered his idol sent word by Ortes de Zarete, a Chilean painter, that he would like to meet Rivera.

MEETING WITH PICASSO

It happened on a day when Rivera was busy in his studio painting a double cubist portrait of two Japanese artists, Tsuguharu Foujita and Riichiro Kawashima. The two were in costume because they were posing for the painting. Zarete rushed in and announced that Pablo Picasso, the most celebrated of the cubist painters, had invited Rivera to come to see him. Work stopped, and all four artists hurried along the streets of Paris to accept the invitation. The two Japanese, in togas and sandals with colorful ribbons tied around their heads, were dressed like characters from an ancient history textbook. The sight of them probably amused many of the people they passed.

Rivera and his friends spent the whole morning in Picasso's studio, absorbed in looking at a powerful display of masterpieces, more than they usually saw at one time. They were also treated to a look at his private sketchbooks. At lunchtime, Zarete and the Japanese artists left, but Picasso asked Rivera to stay. The two cubist painters went to Rivera's studio for a showing of the work he had on hand and then continued their discussion about cubism, its accomplishments and its future, well into the night.

When the other artists in Montparnasse heard that Picasso was enthusiastic about Rivera's work, some were pleased, but others were angered. Rivera expressed his excitement, saying: "Being accepted by the master of cubism himself was, of course, a source of tremendous personal satisfaction to me. Not only did I consider Picasso a great artist, but I respected his critical judgment, which was severe and keen."

ANGELINE AND DIEGO IN SPAIN

Rivera had little time to savor his personal success. World War I broke out in 1914. Life would never again be the same for Angeline and Diego, nor for anyone else. When the fighting broke out, the couple was away from Paris, painting with a group of other artists in Majorca, Spain. They ended up staying on the island for three months. Then with their money all

Like Rivera, many Latin American artists spent the years during World War I in Europe, particularly in Paris and Vienna. This European influence is displayed in Latin American art of the time, as in Rivera's 1914 cubist work *El grande de España (El ángel azul)*. Decades later, however, the Mexican mural movement would show a truly original side of these artists—large-scale political statements that reflected their own unique points of view.

but gone, they sailed to Barcelona. The galleries in Paris closed. For months no artists could exhibit or sell their canvases. The art in demand was mostly related to the war effort. They had to find a way to earn a living.

Angeline accepted a commission for painting the Russian coat of arms on a wall at the Russian consulate. Diego assisted her. She painted the eagle, which was the focal point of the art, and he painted Saint George and the dragon on a shield. The consul was so pleased that he offered them more work, but they accepted the money and bought train tickets to Madrid.

Their stay in Spain lasted nearly a year. Angeline earned a fee for tutoring children in her native language of Russian. She also sold a few small works of her art. Rivera and another artist, María Blanchard, exhibited their cubist paintings, but the more conservative art critics in Madrid were not ready to appreciate this unconventional art. Sales were poor.

BACK TO PARIS DURING THE WAR

In 1915, Rivera returned to a Paris that was far different than the one he left. Angeline followed later. Many of the artists they had known had gone off to war. Some came home to recover from serious wounds; others never came back. Rivera claimed he volunteered to join the French army but was rejected for health reasons. To earn money, he signed a contract with an art dealer, who would buy four of his canvases a month. These sales kept the couple going in wartime Paris when prices skyrocketed. They needed all the money they could get. Rivera painted more quickly than ever, producing cubist still lifes, landscapes, and portraits, sometimes as many as five per month.

Zapatista Landscape (The Guerrilla) was one of the most significant works Rivera did during this time. In fact, it led to his getting a contract with an art dealer. As Rivera described it, "It showed a Mexican peasant hat hanging over a wooden box behind a rifle. Executed without any preliminary sketch in my Paris workshop, it is probably the most faithful expression of the Mexican mood that I have ever achieved."

Rivera considered the painting to be testimony to his progressive politics, "one of the few solid pieces of evidence suggesting that Rivera had displayed revolutionary sympathies when the outcome of the uprising in Mexico was still in the balance," according to Rivera biographer Patrick Marnham. But Rivera's original intent was never that obvious, Marnham suggests, because Rivera didn't initially title the piece. Even a year after he painted it, Rivera referred to it only as "my Mexican trophy."

Nevertheless, in 1916, with a world war raging not far from his Paris studio, that important landscape foreshadowed the emergence of Rivera as a revolutionary painter. His studio was in Europe, but his eye was on the events in his homeland, where the revolution continued. The French press ran numerous photos of Emiliano Zapata, standing fierce and defiant, wearing a sombrero and many gun belts, carrying a rifle and a sword. Zapata, by then a folk hero, was the leader of one of the peasant bands fighting to overthrow the Mexican government. These pictures, taken by Augustín Casasola, must have fired the imagination of Diego Rivera, although his stories of briefly joining Zapata's forces during his 1910 trip to Mexico are probably not true.

RIVERA'S FIRST CHILD

Even in wartime, life goes on. In the summer of 1916, Angeline gave birth to Rivera's son. They named him after his father and called him "Dieguito." Rivera seemed happy and proud to have sired a son, although he had said before the birth that he did not want a baby disrupting his work. Art was always the most important thing in Rivera's life.

Rivera did one cubist portrait of Angeline while she was pregnant and another of her feeding the baby. Around the same time, Rivera began an affair with another Russian artist, Marevna Vorobev, who also posed for several of his paintings. Six years younger than Rivera, she had first been a friend of Angeline's.

Even while in Europe, Rivera remained keenly aware of changes occurring in Mexico. Rivera's portrait of rebel leader Emiliano Zapata shows him armed and ready to overthrow the Mexican government.

Baby Dieguito did not thrive, especially after Angeline left Rivera and moved to a small apartment that had no heat. The baby was undernourished (food, especially milk, was either scarce or expensive during the war), and he had many colds. Rivera was of little help during the five months he lived with

Marevna, a "she-devil" whose beauty and fiery personality he found wildly attractive. But he soon tired of her, partly because of her violent fits, which sometimes resulted in physical attacks, and he returned to Angeline and his son.

Many months afterward, Marevna accused him of fathering the daughter she bore. If so, which seems likely, their affair did not end when Rivera returned to Angeline. The baby, named Marika, was born in November 1919. Years later, Rivera wrote:

> The child Marika, now grown up and married, is a lovely woman and an accomplished dancer. For many reasons, she too wrote me letters and sent me photographs in the hope of softening my flinty old heart. . . . Even if, by the barest chance, I was really her father, neither she nor [her mother] ever actually needed me.

Dieguito lived only 14 months. On a chilly October day in 1917, Rivera and Angeline buried their son in the Montrouge cemetery. Marevna, who wrote that she watched the funeral from a distance, placed flowers next to a small cross bearing the inscription "Diego Rivera."

CONTROVERSY OVER CUBISM

Rivera and Angeline moved to a different apartment, away from the art colony in Montparnasse. Their reasons were both personal and professional. Rivera had become embroiled in a controversy over cubism. Various artists and critics argued continually over exactly what cubism was. Some of the more influential voices opposed Rivera's original theories. He painted "cubist portraits"; his opponents "argued that such a portrait was an impossibility since a portrait was a likeness and cubism was an attempt to reform or reassemble conventional likeness."

This difference of opinion, which seems trivial now, led to a scandal that came to be known as "l'affaire Rivera." After a dinner party, an argument between Rivera and Pierre Reverdy, a poet and art critic, nearly turned violent. After throwing a punch at Reverdy for insulting him, Rivera attempted to apologize. His handshake was refused. No one was hurt, but several witnesses took sides, mostly against Rivera. His art dealer ended up on the opposing side and took most of Rivera's works off the market, including *Zapatista Landscape,* which had figured prominently in the argument.

Picasso, whose genius did not always manifest itself in originality, had a reputation for "stealing" the ideas of painters he knew and often using them to better effect. Rivera had been quite vocal in claiming that Picasso copied two elements from *Zapatista Landscape.* One was the trees, which Rivera did in black and dark green, using a technique called scumbling (applying a thin coat of color and softening lines by rubbing); the other was the white silhouette, or negative space, which was the "shadow" of the rifle in the painting. (In his own works, Picasso later painted over the elements Rivera claimed he copied.)

Feeling more and more like an exile in Paris, Diego Rivera was ready for yet another artistic change. A few months before his son's death, he stopped painting in the cubist style and returned to realism with a simple still life he called *Frutas.* The change began on an ordinary day as he walked away from the gallery of his dealer. He described it later:

> I saw a curbside pushcart filled with peaches. Suddenly, my whole being was filled with this commonplace object. I stood there transfixed, my eyes absorbing every detail. With unbelievable force, the texture, forms, and colors of the peaches seemed to reach out toward me. I rushed back to my studio and began my experiments that very day.

SEARCHING FOR A STYLE

What followed were numerous experiments. For a time he painted in the manner of Cézanne, whose work he greatly admired. Some paintings he thought of as failures. But he persisted, despite his mounting dissatisfaction, even as he listened to the news of the Bolshevik Revolution in Russia. The couple's Russian friends were saying goodbye and making plans to return to their homeland to help build the future. Rivera, whose interest in politics was increasing, considered going to Russia, too. But he realized that what he knew best was his own country. More and more he thought of Mexico.

In his continuing search for a distinctive style, Rivera saw that the world was changing. Nothing would be the same after a war or revolution. He predicted there would be a new society, which he called a "mass society." This new society would need a new art. He wrote, "The new art . . . would not be museum or gallery art but an art the people would have access to in places they frequented in their daily life—post offices, schools, theaters, railroad stations, public buildings. And so . . . I arrived at mural painting."

Rivera had become friends with Élie Faure, an important art critic. The two spent hours discussing art. "Faure divided the history of art into alternating periods dominated by the 'individual' or the 'collective' genius. He argued that the work of Cézanne and Renoir marked the end of an individual period that had started with the Renaissance, and that a new collective period would be born in the twentieth century."

In this new period, Faure believed painters must decorate the walls of public buildings with a form of art that would endure. Fresco was the most long-lasting form of mural painting. So Faure encouraged Rivera to visit the cathedrals of Italy and see the work of Giotto, who had painted in the medieval collective period. Rivera wanted to do exactly that, but he had little money for such a trip. He sold a painting to Alberto Pani, the Mexican ambassador to France. Then the ambassador commissioned Rivera to do portraits of himself and his wife. Their son took painting lessons from the artist. Rivera also did other commissioned portraits. Using his connection with Pani, Rivera contacted the Mexican government and obtained 2,000 pesos along with a presidential order stating that the money was to finance a trip to Italy to study the art of fresco.

Accepting the money also meant agreeing to return to Mexico to work for the government. The new head of the Ministry of Education, a man named José Vasconcelos, planned to teach the illiterate populace of Mexico to read. Reviving mural painting was an essential part of that plan; people who could not read could learn the history of their country by looking at art. Many artists would work under the direction of Vasconcelos to paint the murals that taught the lessons of history.

LEARNING FRESCO IN ITALY

Before Rivera could be one of the artists to create a national art for Mexico, however, he had to learn the craft of painting frescoes, which was practically a lost art. He went to Italy alone.

ÉLIE FAURE

Rivera's friendship with Élie Faure was among his most important. It's not clear when the men first met, but it could have been in about 1918, the year attributed to a reproduction of an oil painting Rivera had done of the French art critic. It was Faure, who began his career as a military medic, who may have been responsible for convincing Rivera to attempt his first female nudes in the style of the French impressionist Pierre-Auguste Renoir, according to biographer Patrick Marnham.

Faure was fond of Rivera. Faure believed Rivera possessed a "monstrous intelligence" and was a great "mythomaniac" who spun enjoyable yarns about Mexico. Rivera respected Faure as well, which is reflected in the portrait showing Faure in his military uniform, his elbow resting on a table next to a bunch of grapes.

(He and Angeline were not getting along.) Bertram Wolfe writes of Rivera's trip to Italy:

> With brushes, paints, a few socks and things in a knapsack, he set off for Italy to see its walls. Seventeen months he spent tramping, drinking in Italy's treasures, making more than three hundred sketches. . . . He found a continual feast for his bulging eyes. What he saw and sketched would leave traces on all his future work.

(Although Rivera claimed he spent 17 months touring Italy, recent biographers believe the time to have been much less.)

The sketches he made show the myriad objects that caught his artistic eye. While studying a fresco by Masaccio, Rivera sketched a muralist's scaffold that stood nearby. "It was a wooden pyramid, five ascending platforms, connected by ladders and mounted on wheels." Other sketches ranged from street scenes in Milan, where everyone spat in public, including elegantly dressed women (a custom Rivera found unattractive), to Etruscan funeral vases and tomb paintings he saw in Tuscany, to mosaics in Ravenna narrating the divine messages of Christianity for the masses.

Perhaps it was the size (six feet by 20 feet) of Paolo Uccello's *Rout of San Romano* in the Uffizi Gallery of Florence that caught Rivera's attention. Rivera sketched the horses and armor of the fresco in fine detail. Of all the old masters of fresco he saw, however, Giotto, as Élie Faure predicted, influenced Rivera the most. Journalist and former art student Pete Hamill remarks that:

> In Giotto . . . we see much of what Rivera's mural style would contain at its best, . . . the beautifully designed massing of figures in some scenes and in others the isolation of figures to evoke a mood of abandonment; the use of common objects such as tables or wine jars to give the viewer a sense of the familiar.

When Rivera returned to Paris filled with new ideas for his art, he said goodbye to Angeline. He promised that as soon as he settled in Mexico, he would send her money so she could join him. He never did. Their relationship ended when he sailed from Le Havre, France, to Veracruz.

In his autobiography, he wrote, "My homecoming produced an esthetic exhilaration which is impossible to describe. It was as if I were being born anew, born into a new world. . . . Gone was the doubt and inner conflict that had tormented me in Europe." When Diego Rivera returned to Mexico at the age of 35, he was ready to become a revolutionary muralist in what art critics would call the Mexican Renaissance.

Early Murals

When Diego Rivera arrived in Mexico City in 1921, he was ready to paint walls. He contacted José Vasconcelos, who had been appointed the minister of education and had the backing of the current president, General Alvaro Obregón. Vasconcelos looked at the portfolio Rivera brought with him. The cubist works did not impress the minister. Neither did Rivera's post-cubist art. Rivera had spent too much time in Europe. He had lost touch with his homeland. Vasconcelos wanted an artist who had experience doing murals (Rivera had none) and, even more important, one who could paint the images of Mexico on walls for all to see.

Vasconcelos assigned a wall in an old church to a rival of Rivera's, an artist named Roberto Montenegro (he had been a student at San Carlos and had been chosen over Rivera for an art scholarship when they were in school together). The best the minister could do for Rivera was to give him a job in the Department of Fine Arts at the university. It was a start.

With his small salary, Rivera could help his aging parents, both of whom were ill. His father died of cancer before the end of the year. Rivera took the loss hard. He held Don Diego in high regard. His mother died in 1923.

In November, Vasconcelos led a group of artists working for the government on a journey to Yucatán. His purpose was to acquaint these men, including Rivera, with their own heritage, the art of ancient Mexico. They toured the ruins of Chichén Itzá and Uxmal. As Rivera's excitement grew, Vasconcelos was pleased. The ex-cubist painter sketched the ruins, sculptures, and artifacts of the pre-Columbian civilization as well as the descendants of the Mayan people who still lived in the region.

FIRST MURAL

Immediately upon his return to Mexico City, Rivera painted two canvases in the style of murals that proved he was beginning to get the message. They are both titled *Balcony in Yucatán*. Using brown flesh tones, shadowy blacks, terra-cotta, and green, Rivera depicted two women and a child on a balcony. Vasconcelos thought these efforts showed promise; he gave Rivera his first wall to paint.

Rivera was put in charge of doing a mural in the Anfiteatro Bolívar, a concert auditorium in the National Preparatory School. He and four assistants (also artists) were to cover a wall at the back of the stage, about 1,000 square feet. Vasconcelos had told them he wanted a "universal theme." Rivera wrote later:

> The subject of the mural was *Creation*, which I symbolized as everlasting and the core of human history. More specifically, I presented a racial history of Mexico through figures representing all the types that had entered the Mexican blood stream,

Upon returning to Mexico, Rivera began to concentrate on painting local subjects and adapting his style to mural painting. This detail from a larger mural featuring Tehuna Indian women reflects the artist's passion for the people of his homeland.

from the autochthonous [or native] Indian to the present-day, half-breed Spanish Indian.

But Rivera and his team did not achieve all they attempted. Few viewers were satisfied with the resulting mural that took more than a year to complete. Perhaps there were too many technical problems to solve. Rivera had to incorporate both an arch and an antique pipe organ into the design of the mural. With the colors he used on the arch, he suggested a rainbow. The organ became part of the trunk of the *Tree of Life* (later, officials replaced the organ with a canopy, displaying the arms of the university).

It took time for Rivera to draw 20 figures to scale as well as to teach himself to paint while standing on a scaffold. Then there was the not-so-small matter of what technique to use. Rivera chose encaustic perhaps because he had tried it once before while working in Toledo, and he thought it would last the longest. Vasconcelos also wanted it used. But Rivera had not used it before to paint murals, and it proved to be time-consuming, a bad choice for a big project. In encaustic technique, pigment is first mixed with wax and resin. After it is painted on the wall, it must be heated, then allowed to cool. Rivera's team of assistants used blowtorches to keep the walls the right temperature. Learning how to manage a team of assistants was another problem to be solved while doing this first mural.

Creation did not have enough of the character of Mexico to suit Vasconcelos, so before Rivera completed the *Tree of Life* section of the project, the minister sent him on another trip. This time he went to Tehuantepec in the state of Oaxaca. On this journey, Rivera would not only understand the message; he would never forget it. He would make it his own.

In a simple, natural setting, Rivera watched the Indians going about their daily routine and not modeling for him. The ritual of an Indian woman, bathing in a stream bordered by tropical plants, gave him the idea to use the colors, shapes, and subjects that would become his trademark in painting his subsequent portraits of Mexico.

Rivera began to paint *The Bather of Tehuantepec* on canvas. Then he returned to Mexico City to complete his first mural. Among the leaves of the *Tree of Life*, which is a common image from Mexican folk art, he painted an eagle, ox, lion, and caribou. The colors, including the green of the rubbery, tropical leaves on this section of the mural, are evidence that he had finally found his signature style.

Like many of Rivera's later murals, this one sparked controversy. Some people thought it ugly, calling it an outrage; others praised it. Rivera felt dissatisfaction with the work because it was "too metaphorical and subjective for the masses."

Creation had provided a training ground, however. Now Rivera was ready to begin a masterpiece. Nothing would interfere, not even two important events in his personal life.

MARRIAGE TO LUPE MARÍN

The first of these events was marriage to Guadalupe Marín from Guadalajara. Lupe had been his model for three of the figures in his first mural. The details of their meeting had become legend. A mutual friend and beautiful singer, Concha Michel, introduced them in Rivera's studio. The way the story goes, Concha was protecting herself from making a big mistake. If she could interest Diego in Lupe, then she herself would not be tempted to run away with him.

At their first meeting and for the rest of his life, Diego thought Lupe was the ideal of feminine beauty. She had long black hair and transparent green eyes. Slim with round shoulders and muscular legs, she stood six feet tall. Her face reminded him of an Indian's. Her lips were full and her teeth were straight. Her hands were strong and beautiful, like eagle talons.

Lupe was less impressed with him and asked, "Is this the great Diego Rivera? . . . To me he looks horrible!" But she

In the 1920s, Rivera became involved in the Communist Party in Mexico. Like many other Mexican artists and intellectuals of the time, Rivera believed that the radical ideas of Karl Marx and Vladimir Lenin *(above)* would improve the lives of working people in the country.

posed for him immediately. While she ate the fruit he had in a bowl on his worktable, he painted her portrait, then sketched her head and her hands. He was fascinated by her hands and painted them many times after that.

According to Diego, Lupe proposed to him in public at a political meeting. He accepted, and they were married in her hometown in a Catholic church in June 1922. She would bear him two daughters, Guadalupe (1924) and Ruth (1927).

POLITICS

At about that same time, Rivera was attending a number of political meetings. He had joined the Mexican Communist Party. During his long stay in Europe, Rivera had shown little interest in becoming a Communist. But he had heard much talk about Marxism. His common-law wife, Angeline, whom he had abandoned in Paris, was Russian; they had many Russian friends, who had gone home after the Bolshevik Revolution. After the fighting had stopped in the Mexican Revolution, many of the artists, writers, and intellectuals of the day were discussing Marxist-Leninist ideology. They said publicly that Mexico would benefit if it adopted this ideology in the same way they thought the Soviet Union had.

Rivera quickly became a leader in the party as well as the president of a union he helped organize along with several artists. The artists of the Revolutionary Union of Technical Workers, Painters and Sculptors wanted to think of themselves as workers, that is, plasterers and craftsmen in the building trades fighting in a class struggle.

Eventually, Rivera's role in both groups came to be that of a celebrity. He and Lupe, an excellent cook, often entertained important people in their home, which she had decorated with wood and leather furniture, straw mats, Indian blankets, and Rivera's cubist paintings. Diego, always the storyteller, talked a lot and never rejected a chance to answer questions posed by reporters, when any were present. He enjoyed participating in the world of ideas. Frida Kahlo later observed that Rivera was irritated only by two things: "loss of time from work—and stupidity." He would rather have "many intelligent enemies than one stupid friend," his future wife once said. But when there was controversy, he protected himself, his art, and his career.

A DIFFICULT ART COMMISSION

One of the guests in Rivera and Marín's home was Vasconcelos, who chose Diego Rivera to decorate the walls of the new Ministry of Education Building in Mexico City. Rivera would be the primary artist and would be in charge of the team of assistant artists and plasterers. It was an important project, and it was huge—235 panels of fresco, 15,000 square feet, on the walls of three floors in two open courtyards, the walls of

Diego's wife and muse, Lupe Marín, represented the ideal of feminine beauty for him. Lupe posed for him many times, and she bore him two daughters. Their marriage yielded much inspiration and creativity for Rivera, but Lupe eventually divorced him because of his extramarital affairs.

a stairway, and the hall leading to the elevator. It took Rivera and his team four years to complete the work.

From the beginning, Rivera, however, realized that if they used the time-consuming encaustic technique again, the project would take far longer than that. He switched to fresco. But he and his team knew very little about it. They researched the methods used in frescoes around the world (this included the method used by Giotto, the master whose art Rivera had admired on his tour of Italy), and they studied a book written by Cennino Cennini in 1400 about *buon fresco* as used in Italy. Then they tried it.

LEARNING FRESCO

Results varied. Some days the plaster dried too quickly. Adding more water to the mixture made the paint watery, too. Not long after work began on the huge project, one of the team artists, Jean Charlot, was leaving the dark building late at night after working all day. He walked by Rivera's scaffold and saw that it was quivering. He compared it with the start of an earthquake. Looking up in the dim light, he could make out Rivera's huge body. Charlot climbed the scaffold and found Rivera picking away at his day's work, scraping off the painted plaster with a hand trowel. The quality of the work was not up to his exacting standards. Crying like a child throwing a temper tantrum, the great artist was in despair. Other team members reported similar scenes in the first days of the project. This technical problem was almost too much for Rivera to bear. He felt that he had to master the fresco technique or suffer the worst failure of his career.

Another of Rivera's assistants, Xavier Guerrero, an Indian from Guadalajara, experimented until he found a solution, which Rivera adopted for a time. Guerrero's father, a house painter, had re-created a stucco mixture, like the one the Aztec builders used in the 600-year-old temples of Teotihuacán. It worked better than anything they had previously tried. Always ready with a story, Rivera told the press. When the story ran, it made headlines. The credit went to Rivera for rediscovering a "secret" of the Aztecs. It turned out that the secret was one of the ingredients of the plaster mixture, nopal juice, which is the fermented juice of cactus pads. Although it made for good press, the formula did not quite do the job because the juice, being organic, eventually decomposed and left unsightly stains. More experiments led to a better formula, but that story did not make news.

Rivera gave these details of the trial-and-error period in his autobiography: "I found that for best results, the lime I used had to be burned over a fire made only with wood and then stored in rubber bags for three months. The rubber keeps the lime from absorbing carbon dioxide from the air. . . . Before painting, I have my helpers prepare a surface of three or four plaster coats, the last a mixture of lime with fine marble dust." Eventually, Rivera and his skilled assistants solved the technical problems. Then he was able not only to complete the murals at the Ministry of Education but also to use the same process in future frescoes.

COMPLETING THE MURAL AT THE MINISTRY OF EDUCATION

The Labors and Festivals of the Mexican People that Rivera and his team painted on the walls of the Ministry of Education building is truly a masterpiece. "The murals . . . make up a visual ballad of Mexico, resembling the traditional *corrido*, a narrative in song. . . . Past, present, and future are combined on those walls in a synthesis that came from Diego Rivera. Through the force of his art, he combined dreams, battles, heroes, villains into a new vision of Mexico."

Rivera planned the murals around two general subjects. He designated one courtyard to be the Court of Labor and the other to be the Court of Fiestas. In the Court of Labor, he painted frescoes depicting various types of labor done in Mexico from industrial to agricultural, from scientific to artistic. In the Court of Fiestas, he showed the people of Mexico celebrating their traditional holidays. These included Indian festivals, such as *The Corn Festival*, *The Deer Dance*, and *The Ribbon Dance*, as well as three *Day of the Dead* panels and a panel called *The Burning of the Judases*, a festival at which effigies (dummies) of unpopular figures are set on fire.

Four of the connecting panels in the second court, however, depict a festival that was not a realistic representation of a Mexican fiesta. The *May Day Meeting*, for example, is pure propaganda. In the 1920s, labor unions occasionally marched on May Day in Mexico, but their activity in no way resembled the scene Rivera created, featuring hundreds of factory workers and farmers celebrating beneath red banners that carry the message that Communism will triumph.

Before he finished the murals at the Ministry of Education, Diego Rivera had become one of the most famous Communists in Mexico. By 1927, his fame had spread to the Soviet Union. Communist leaders were preparing to celebrate the tenth anniversary of the October Revolution. They invited celebrities from around the world to attend. Rivera accepted his invitation and left for Moscow, where it was hinted that he, a guest artist, might paint a mural in the Red Army Club ("Red" means Communist).

6

Marriage of the "Red" Artists

Rivera's trip to the Soviet Union interrupted his work on the murals at the Ministry of Education. He stayed in Moscow for eight months, but his most vivid memories centered on his first impression. As one of the visiting dignitaries, he sat on the reviewing stand in Red Square for three hours in freezing November winds, making sketches of an anniversary procession.

After sketching the procession in Red Square, Rivera caught a cold that turned to pneumonia, and he was hospitalized. During his stay in the Communist country, he made 45 sketches and watercolors. Later, Mrs. John D. Rockefeller, Jr., bought the series, called "The May Day Sketches," for the Museum of Modern Art in New York. He lectured young Russian artists on mural painting, sketched Stalin making a speech (Stalin autographed the back of the sketch), and signed a contract to paint a mural in the Red Army Club. When he

During a visit to the Soviet Union, Rivera observed a grand procession through Red Square, an event he likened to a great locomotive leading a giant train. Though Rivera's visit was productive, he was expelled for supporting dissident artists and painters who were being persecuted.

realized that the Communist leaders had no intention of allowing him to paint the mural, he supported a group of dissident artists and a union of painters who were being persecuted. He was asked to leave the country, which he did rather hastily.

MEXICO AND MORE MURALS

Within five months after Rivera returned to Mexico, he completed the frescoes in the Ministry of Education building.

Despite public controversy over Rivera's desire to include a leftist poem (Vasconcelos overrode the artist; the poem was removed) and disagreement among the workers, the work is a masterpiece. Rivera caused some of the disagreement when he had a panel by Jean Charlot chipped off a wall and he repainted it himself.

But some critics as well as painters believe that Rivera's best achievement in public art is the fresco cycle he did from 1924 to 1926 at the chapel of the University of Chapingo in the state of Mexico. Amazingly, he was painting at the ministry at the same time. His work schedule during those years would have seemed impossible to anyone who did not possess his unbounded energy. He worked three long days a week at the ministry then traveled about 40 minutes each way to the campus of the agricultural school outside Mexico City to work three more long days.

Rivera titled the Chapingo frescoes *Song to the Liberated Land*. The space encompassed an entrance hall, stairway, and chapel—nearly 1,500 square feet. Bertram Wolfe writes of Rivera's ability to paint such large areas:

> Many painters . . . are amazed by the virtuosity with which he solved the problems of the complicated spatial structure. . . . In accordance with the uses of the building, he chose themes related to agriculture; the evolution of the earth, germination, growth, florescence, and fruition of plants, and symbolic parallels in the evolution of society. The whole grows from natural and social chaos to harmony, culminating in the harmony of man with nature and man with man.

In these frescoes, Rivera painted nudes to symbolize the virgin Earth, Nature, the fecund (fertile) Earth, and other ideas. His wife, Lupe, posed for many of them. She was pregnant twice while Rivera worked at Chapingo, and Rivera painted her as the fecund Earth to show the fruitfulness of the land. Another model whom Rivera painted nude was Tina Modotti, the Italian photographer who was then living in Mexico. She often traveled with him or met him at Chapingo while the work was being completed. Lupe became very jealous, especially when she discovered that Rivera was having an affair with Tina. After many quarrels over the artist's infidelity, the couple divorced.

FRIDA AND DIEGO

Rivera stayed single for a time, seeing many women. Despite his bulk and lack of traditional good looks, he captivated the opposite sex. In 1929, when he did marry for a third time, it was to Frida Kahlo, who was 21 years younger than he was. She was small, five-foot-three, and weighed about 100 pounds. He was large, six feet tall, and weighed about 300 pounds. The main interests Diego and Frida had in common were their politics (both were members of the Mexican Communist Party) and art.

Pete Hamill describes Kahlo as "sassy, independent, tomboyish, with a unique, striking beauty: glistening intelligent eyes, brows that touched above her nose, sensual lips." Rivera had obvious reasons to be attracted to Kahlo, but together, the large man and petite woman made an unusual match. It was said that their "wedding ceremony was like the marriage of an elephant and a dove."

By one of Frida's perhaps embellished accounts, the couple had their first encounter while Kahlo was a student at the National Preparatory School and Rivera was painting the murals there. Frida, just a teenager at the time, found that she had a crush on the older artist. But in their own writings, Rivera and Kahlo relay stories about an exchange Kahlo had with Rivera while he was working on his scaffold at the Ministry of Education. The young artist wanted Rivera to give her an honest critique of her paintings.

Rivera said that right away he noticed Frida's fine body, long hair, and thick, dark eyebrows, like "the wings of a blackbird" above her nose. When he climbed down, she showed him three of her paintings, portraits of women. He was impressed with their energy, honesty, and personality. He could see "that this girl was an authentic artist" and was delighted with her art. But before he could compliment her, she said she had not come for compliments. She had been warned that he had a reputation for being very friendly to women. What she wanted was his honest opinion of her work. Should she continue painting? Or should she change to some other line of work?

He immediately assured her that she should continue to paint. She said she would follow his advice, and then she asked him to come to her house on Sunday. She wanted him to see more of her work. He accepted the invitation and began seeing her on a regular basis, making frequent trips to her family home, Casa Azul (the Blue House) in Coyoacán on the outskirts of Mexico City.

Kahlo conveyed a similar version of this alleged meeting. "Look, I have not come to flirt or anything even if you are a woman-chaser," she recalled telling him at the Ministry of Education. "I have come to show you my painting." Having reviewed her work, Rivera decided he liked her self-portrait best because it was the most original, Kahlo said. He instructed the young artist to paint something new, which she did, and Rivera was impressed with the results. Kahlo says this marked the beginning of the couple's legendary romantic and artistic relationship.

Despite these anecdotes there's another, more likely, explanation of the meeting that led to the couple's romance, says Kahlo biographer Hayden Herrera. It is one Frida relayed shortly before her 1954 death and suggests the two artists met at a party hosted by Tina Modotti. It would have been a lively gathering, replete with the singing, dancing, and discussions of radical politics common at all of Modotti's weekly events. As Kahlo recalled them, the parties' revelry often spilled out into the streets. "The meeting [with Diego] took place in the period when people carried pistols and went around shooting the street lamps on Madero Avenue and getting into mischief," Frida explained in an article appearing in *Excelsior*, a daily newspaper in Mexico City. "During the night, they broke them

Rivera met artist Frida Kahlo when she was just a student. Although on the surface they seemed ill-suited, their passion for politics and art created a union that could not be broken, despite countless tragedies and betrayals.

all and went about spraying bullets, just for fun. . . . Diego shot a phonograph and I began to be very interested in him in spite of the fear I had of him."

"THE ELEPHANT AND THE DOVE"

As the two artists began seeing more and more of each other—Rivera visiting Kahlo in Coyoacán and Kahlo visting Rivera on his scaffold—Rivera's ex-wife Lupe Marín became jealous. She didn't like the way Kahlo called Rivera by a pet name, *mi cuatacho* ("my big pal"). She also found one of Kahlo's behaviors to be "very disagreeable." When she and Rivera had gone to visit the young girl, Marín recalled, Kahlo was drinking tequila "like a real mariachi."

Since he was more than twice her age, many people, including some in Kahlo's own family, wondered about Diego's intentions. Frida's father, Don Guillermo Kahlo, a German photographer, asked Diego if he was interested in his daughter. When Diego admitted he was, Don Guillermo said, "She is a devil." Diego replied that he knew, and Don Guillermo said, "Well, I've warned you." Then Don Guillermo left the room, and Diego believed he had gotten tacit approval of the match. On the other hand, Frida's mother, who was a Catholic, did not approve of her daughter marrying a Communist.

From the beginning of their relationship, Frida was the most important person in Diego's life, although their years together were often stormy and included ill health, miscarriages, divorce, remarriage, and infidelities. Diego had affairs with many women, including Frida's sister, Cristina; Frida had affairs with both men and women.

Like many of the women Diego met, Frida posed for Diego's paintings, but not as many as his previous wives. Even before they married, she became the model for the panel titled *Distributing Arms at the Ministry of Education*. In it, she is dressed in a red shirt and black skirt. Her hair is shorn, making her look boyish. She and Tina Modotti, also in red and black, are handing out rifles and ammunition in the revolutionary struggle.

For a great deal of her life, Frida was in pain. One of her legs was disfigured by polio when she was six, and she was seriously injured in a streetcar accident when she was 17. The streetcar accident left her unable to bear children. The day they got married, Don Guillermo reportedly gave Diego a final warning. "Now, look, my daughter is a sick person and all her life she's going to be sick," he said. "She's intelligent but not pretty. Think it over if you like, and if you still wish to marry her, marry her. I give you my permission."

Kahlo and Rivera got married in a civil ceremony at Coyoacán's city hall on August 21, 1929. A newspaper article appearing in the Mexico City *La Prensa* noted its "unpretentious" nature. Kahlo had worn only "simple street clothes." Rivera wore a suit without a vest. In the wedding photo accompanying the piece, Kahlo's relaxed attitude is evident: In her right hand, the new bride is holding a cigarette.

As laid-back as the ceremony may have been, the wedding party was anything but. One of the guests, Rivera's ex-wife Lupe Marín, caused a huge stir, according to Rivera biographer Bertram Wolfe. Apparently hoping to humiliate Rivera and Kahlo, she unexpectedly lifted Frida's skirt and shouted an insult: "You see these two sticks? These are the legs Diego has now instead of mine?"

Frida never relayed that story herself, though she did recall some bad behavior on the part of her new husband. "Diego went on such a terrifying drunken binge with tequila that he took out his pistol, he broke a man's little finger, and broke other things. Then we had a fight, and I left crying and went home," Frida remembered.

Not long after the couple wed, Diego paid off the mortgage on Casa Azul, allowing Frida's parents to continue living in the house where Frida had been born, where she would live for part of her married life, and where she would die in 1954.

Diego and Frida, meanwhile, made their home at a majestic house on one of Mexico City's most refined streets, the Paseo de la Reforma. With its French Gothic-style façade and entranceway that Rivera had decorated with pre-Columbian figures, it displayed a mix of cultural influences. Along with a live-in maid, Diego and Frida shared the residence with the

Rivera raises his fist in the Communist salute during Mexican Labor's anti-fascist demonstration in Mexico City on November 23, 1936. Kahlo stands next to him. Both artists were active members of the Communist Party.

painter and fervent Stalinist David Alfaro Siqueiros; his wife, Blanca Luz Brum; and two other communists.

Indeed, these were eventful times. The year Diego married Frida, the couple's mutual friend Tina Modotti had fallen in love with an exiled Cuban Communist, Julio Antonia Mella, who was working to overthrow the dictator of Cuba, Gerardo Machado. One night in January as Mella and Tina were walking home from a meeting, a Machado assassin killed Mella. When Tina became a suspect in the murder, Rivera successfully defended her.

EXPELLED FROM THE COMMUNIST PARTY

But his defense of a comrade did not help Rivera win the approval of party leaders in Moscow. The Stalinists in the Soviet Union demanded strict allegiance of their members. Rivera had not been good at following their rules. As a guest of the government during his visit to celebrate the tenth anniversary of the revolution, he had been expelled from the country. Back in Mexico, he had accepted commissions to paint murals on the walls of government buildings, and he served as director of the San Carlos Academy, the art school he had attended as a youth—another government position. The Communist Party was working toward the overthrow of the Mexican government. But Diego Rivera seemed to be in support of this government, and so he was expelled from the Mexican Communist Party a few weeks after he and Frida were married.

Frida's friend from the National Preparatory School, Baltasar Dromundo, laid out a colorful account of the scene:

> Diego arrived, sat down, and took out a large pistol and put it on a table. He then put a handkerchief over the pistol and said: "I, Diego Rivera, general secretary of the Mexican Communist party, accuse the painter Diego Rivera of collaborating with the petit-bourgeois government of Mexico and of having accepted a commission to paint the stairway of the National Palace of Mexico. This contradicts the politics of the Comintern and

therefore the painter Diego Rivera should be expelled from the Communist party by the general secretary of the Communist party, Diego Rivera."

It was then that Diego stood up, declared himself expelled, removed the handkerchief and shattered the gun. It was made of clay.

While Frida resigned in solidarity with her husband, Diego's former comrades refused to have anything to do with him. They included people like Tina Modotti, those he considered to be his friends. He tried to make light of the situation, joking that he had voted for his own expulsion, but in reality he took it hard. He suffered a nervous breakdown.

Artist of All Mexico

Shortly before Rivera suffered the nervous breakdown in 1929, he had accepted a commission "to decorate the main staircase of the historic National Palace in Zócalo, probably the most prestigious site for a fresco in the whole of Mexico."

After recovering his health, he continued this staircase project, *History of Mexico*. Years later (1942), Rivera began, but did not complete, another fresco cycle, *Prehispanic and Colonial Mexico* in the first-floor corridors of the palace. This monumental work was interrupted several times while he completed other murals in both Mexico and the United States. In his autobiography, Rivera said he put the final touches on his stairway mural at the palace in 1955, more than 20 years after he started. His friends often teased him about taking so long.

Rivera made light of the situation, but he probably welcomed interruptions, at least in the beginning. In Mexico City, he and his murals at the National Palace were under attack from many critics. Some citizens disliked his Communist leanings, despite his expulsion from the party, whereas his former comrades viewed him as a traitor for painting government walls. Meanwhile, he resigned from his directorship at San Carlos because both professors and students opposed the reforms he tried to make in the curriculum. When he defended his murals in the press, threats from architectural students who wanted to deface his frescoes resulted in his carrying pistols and cartridge belts onto his scaffold as he worked. His team of assistants also acted as guards.

On the walls of the presidential palace, Rivera painted the myths, legends, religions, cultures, enemies, wars, arts, crafts, architecture, and people of Mexico. To portray all of Mexican history from ancient times to the year he started his sketches, he began with the Aztec deity, Quetzalcóatl, appearing in both human form and as plumed serpent. He depicted the downfall of the Aztec civilization. He painted the era from the Spanish Conquest through colonial times to independence from Spain. Moving on, he included the invasion by the United States (1847), the reign of Maximilian, the period known as the Porfiriato, the Revolution (beginning in 1910), and all the presidents from Madero to Calles. In the final panel, he depicted a utopian future as envisioned by Diego Rivera: The people seize control to follow the Communist teachings of Karl Marx.

INTERVENING MURAL COMMISSIONS

Two mural commissions interrupted Rivera's work on the palace staircase: *Health and Life* in the Ministry of Health and *History of Cuernavaca and Morelos* in the Palace of Cortés in Cuernavaca in the state of Morelos. The second was the more controversial. Commissioned as a goodwill gesture by Dwight Morrow, the U.S. ambassador to Mexico, this mural and Rivera's decision to paint it displeased the leaders of the Communist Party once again. Morrow paid about $12,000 for the work from his personal funds and left the theme up to Rivera.

The artist chose to continue his work with Mexican history on three second-floor walls of an open corridor, which faced two volcanoes, Iztaccihuatl and Popocatépetl, in the Valley

Rivera's Communist beliefs cost him dearly. The mural at Mexico's Hotel Reforma *(above)* was one of many criticized for its political content. Shortly after this photograph was taken in December 1936, Rivera was arrested.

of Mexico. In 16 panels, he showed the history of the state of Morelos from the Spanish Conquest to the building of sugar refineries. His final panel, depicting Emiliano Zapata leading the peasant revolt, is perhaps the most memorable, certainly the most famous. Pete Hamill writes that "Rivera's portrait of Zapata, a machete [sugar-cane cutter] in his right hand, his left holding the reins of a white horse, is the best of his many portrayals of the man from Morelos who had come during the Revolution to conquer Cuernavaca itself. That Zapata portrait remains part of the Mexican imagination to this day."

The fresco at Cuernavaca is a Rivera masterpiece. It is the artistic achievement of a master, one who must have dreamed of creating such a work when, as a young man, he toured Italy to study the art of fresco. This masterpiece had a lasting effect on Rivera, artistically and personally. Writes biographer Patrick Marnham, "In Cuernavaca Rivera discovered the theme that was to mark his work more than any other; he . . . detected the key to his own identity as a painter and as a man, and it lay in his treatment of the Mexican Indians." His interest in the ancient and modern Indians of Mexico, their art and architecture, intensified. Rivera collected more of their stone idols; he had started his collection after his first trip to Tehuantepec. He bought Tehuana Indian clothing, jewelry, and other ornaments for Frida. At first, she wore them like costumes to please him. Later, they became her signature style in dress, even when she traveled outside Mexico to San Francisco, Detroit, New York, and Paris with Diego or to show her art. Rivera began the work at the Palace of Cortés in January and finished in September of 1930.

The time he and Frida spent as newlyweds in Ambassador Morrow's villa, Casa Mañana, was a happy time. Cuernavaca (as Rivera's biographer Marnham noted) was associated with Xochiquetzal, the goddess of love, in the days of the Aztecs. While there, Rivera made a drawing of Frida wearing only the Indian beads she is unclasping from her neck. It was the only nude he did of her.

The month after Rivera completed the Cuernavaca work, he and Frida traveled to San Francisco. He would paint two major frescoes in that city and thoroughly enjoy his stay in California. Frida, on the other hand, did not much care for the country she called "Gringolandia." She suffered from back and foot pain caused by her streetcar accident and childhood polio. And she was recovering from a miscarriage. *Indian Woman Nude* and a self-portrait in Tehuana dress, two of the paintings she did in San Francisco, clearly show her husband's influence and her growing interest in Indian themes.

Rivera reveled in the treatment he received from his generous hosts. For him it was fiesta time. He lectured. He showed his art. And he made friends with the rich and famous, including Helen Wills Moody, a tennis champion who became his model for the mural *Allegory of California*. He did this mural at the Pacific Stock Exchange, a project suggested by San Francisco architect Timothy Pflueger. Moody appears twice in the fresco, first as a huge mother figure, symbolizing sunny California, and then as a smaller, flying nude.

The piece is composed of images of the state's industry, natural resources, and workers, including miners looking for gold. Two historical figures are also portrayed—James Marshall, the man who discovered gold in California, and Luther Burbank, the state's famed horticulturist (plant researcher).

While some critics at the time saw the mural as a testament to the state's "riches" and "fertility" and a celebration of the workers who tapped into it, others believe Rivera's intent was more critical. Public art scholar Hilde Hein says it "suggested a disrupted relationship among the land, its economy, and its laboring forces." Most of California's land "was owned by wealthy absentee landlords and cultivated by unskilled immigrants," she points out. Another art scholar, Anthony W. Lee, notes that several of the natural resources depicted in the mural are actually depleted. "The pathetic stump of a tree, for example, does not hint at a dense, limitless redwood forest. . . . The gold for which Marshall pans had run out in California long ago, and we are left with his portrait as a sign of wealth no longer attainable."

Rivera's other major work is a 40-by-30-foot panel on the north wall of the San Francisco Art Institute. When the art was commissioned, it was made clear that the subject should be suitable for an art school and must not have a political theme. Rivera obliged in record time—two months—with *The Making of a Fresco, Showing the Building of a City.* Hamill writes, "The mural's great charm comes from its dominating design element: Rivera himself, seated on a painted scaffold with his back to the viewer, palette in one hand, brush in another, while four assistants labor on other aspects of the mural. The painted wall is about constructing the modern city, but it is also about constructing the modern mural. . . . This is a happy piece of work."

Happy indeed. And humorous, considering how Rivera has depicted his substantial rear end drooping over the scaffold near the center of the painting. Below him are Pflueger, San Francisco Art Commission President William Gerstle, and Arthur Brown Jr., architect for the school (then known as the California School of Fine Arts), huddled together in their business suits, poring over what are presumably architectural plans.

Not everyone was keen on Rivera putting his posterior on display. A painter named Kenneth Callahan suggested that "many San Franciscans chose to see in this gesture a direct insult, premeditated as it appears to be. If it is a joke, it is a rather amusing one, but in bad taste."

The day after Rivera finished this work, he and Frida returned to Mexico, where they stayed in the Blue House in Coyoacán. Meanwhile, Diego arranged to have the couple's new home built in San Angel. It was an unusual setup, with two studios and living quarters—"his and hers" houses— connected by a bridge. Diego immediately went back to work on the stairway at the palace; officials were impatient for him to finish. He completed work on the west wall.

Rivera returned to San Francisco a virtual celebrity. He lectured, showed his work, and socialized with the wealthy. Kahlo was less impressed with the industrialized United States, calling it "Gringolandia."

MURAL COMMISSIONS AND CENSORSHIP IN THE UNITED STATES

Rivera's next trip north of the border kept him out of the country for more than two years. New York was his first stop for a one-man retrospective at the Museum of Modern Art. The preparations for the elaborate show took time and energy. He framed and hung nearly 150 paintings, drawings, and watercolors. Since his murals could not be transported and displayed, he duplicated several from the Ministry of Education and from Cuernavaca on portable panels. And he did three new works after he arrived in New York: *Pneumatic Drillers*, *Power*, and *Frozen Assets*.

The show was a smash hit, even bigger than the museum's first one-man show of Henri Matisse's art. Crowds swelled to more than 57,000 in a month. "The Rockefellers turned out in force, as did the other princely families of Manhattan, the crowd of millionaires and celebrities who patronized modern art: the Goodyears, the Blisses, the Crowninshields, with Georgia O'Keeffe, Edward G. Robinson, Greta Garbo, Hedy Lamar and Paul Robeson," Marnham wrote in his Rivera biography. Diego Rivera was at the top of his game. Ironically, Rivera's success in 1931 occurred when the Depression plagued the United States with homelessness, soup kitchens, breadlines, starvation, and suicides.

Fresh from Diego's personal success, Diego and Frida headed for his next commission at the art institute in Detroit. There he triumphed over controversy. Later, however, when he was back in New York to paint the wall in the lobby of the RCA Building for the Rockefellers, Diego Rivera suffered his biggest defeat. After being told to stop work on a masterpiece, he was paid off and escorted from the building. He was being censored for his Communist themes.

An anti-Stalinist Communist group led by one of Rivera's friends, his biographer Bertram D. Wolfe, offered Rivera some other work, inviting him to paint a history of the United States on 21 movable panels at the New Workers School building in New York City. Having been kicked out of Rockefeller Center months earlier, Rivera wasn't in the most productive of moods—at least when it came to painting. He did manage to muster up the energy to research his project, however, deliver art and political lectures, and address the audience at a student protest at Columbia University. The demonstration, which Frida Kahlo attended with her husband, had been spurred by the university's dismissal of a Communist economics instructor.

As expected, Rivera and Kahlo's New York apartment bustled with visitors, whom Diego often entertained at local restaurants. He took a particular liking to Louise Nevelson, a beautiful Russian-born sculptor in her 30's. As he spent more time with Nevelson, his marriage to Frida began to suffer. Not only was Kahlo feeling lonely (and not well, as her right foot felt paralyzed), but she was also yearning to go back to Mexico. Rivera, on the other hand, enjoyed the support he received from the Manhattan art world and believed that the Communist cause would better be served in the United States. An industrialized country, after all, would be a more likely spot for world revolution.

Arguments ensued over where the couple should live. In an especially heated dustup witnessed by Lucienne Bloch and Stephen Dimitroff, one of Diego's assistants, Diego held up his painting of desert cacti and shouted: "I don't want to go back to that!" Kahlo responded that she, in fact, *did* wish to return to her home country, and Rivera reportedly responded by grabbing a kitchen knife and slicing his painting to bits. According to one of Bloch's diary entries, Kahlo took this as a "gesture of hate towards Mexico."

Rivera eventually finished his New Workers School frescoes in early December. Falling back on an earlier promise—to spend all of his Rockefeller earnings painting revolutionary murals in the United States—he painted two small panels at the New York City Trotsky headquarters at Union Square.

Man, Controller of the Universe, a smaller and slightly altered version of the mural intended for Rockefeller Center, was displayed in the Palace of Fine Arts in Mexico. The work portrays man at a crossroads of industry, science, capitalism, and Communism. In this version, Rivera retained the portrait of Lenin at the bottom right corner.

Sufficiently broke, he prepared to return to Mexico, his *Man at the Crossroads* mural awaiting its destiny of being smashed into bits of tiny plaster the following year.

BACK TO MEXICO

When Diego and Frida returned to Mexico, they moved into their new house in San Angel. Actually, *houses* would be a more apt term, given the separate living arrangements. Frida's headquarters, located in the blue building, were smaller and more private than those of Rivera, a pink building that included a huge kitchen and a studio with high ceilings. A bridge connected the studio to Frida's rooftop terrace. According to Bertram Wolfe's wife, Ella Wolfe, Diego built the two separate cubic-shaped structures because "it seemed, from a bohemian point of view, the 'interesting' or 'arresting' thing to do." But biographer Herrera points to an alternate explanation. She cites a Mexican newspaper article suggesting that "[Diego's] architectural theories are based on the Mormon concept of life, that is to say, the objective and subjective interrelationships that exist between the casa grande and the casa chica!" (The "big house" in Mexico refers to a man's home, she explains. The "little house" is the apartment for a mistress.)

Several months passed before Rivera, who'd been suffering from depression and ill health, began sketching and painting Indian and Mexican themes again. In November, the Mexican government offered him a wall in the Palace of Fine Arts (Palacio de Bellas Artes) for the reconstruction of his RCA mural. He did the fresco quickly (it is smaller than the original) and changed the title to *Man, Controller of the Universe*. Other changes were slight. The head of John D. Rockefeller, Jr., is placed near an enlargement of syphilis bacteria. A portrait of Rivera's friend, biographer, and comrade, Bertram Wolfe, appears between Marx and Trotsky. Lenin, whose portrait caused the censorship of the original mural, is a prominent figure.

Because the only Mexican subjects in the fresco are a parrot, a rubber tree, and a hairless dog, some viewers feel the work is inappropriate for the space. It may have been a hollow victory for Rivera to redo the painting in Mexico, but it is there for visitors to see and perhaps ask to hear the story of the original mural's censorship in the United States.

After finishing the reconstruction, he worked on the south wall in the staircase of the National Palace. And he did a four-panel mural for the banquet hall of Alberto Pani's Hotel Reforma. When finished, this mural was censored, but in a different manner than the RCA mural. The title of the work tells its theme: *A Burlesque of Mexican Folklore and Politics*. Pani, a longtime patron of Rivera's and a private citizen, paid for the art, but he did not approve of the finished product because of its attack on contemporary government officials and its message that tourism was ruining Mexico. His hotel, where the mural was to be displayed, catered to tourists. So Pani had his brother repaint certain portions. Rivera took the case to court and won. Changing the art with the artist's signature still on it was ruled a forgery. Pani paid a fine. The murals, which were on movable panels, were sold to a dealer and not displayed for years. Today, they are in the Palacio de Bellas Artes.

POLITICS AND PAINTING INDIAN THEMES

No walls were offered to Rivera for some time after that. He had displeased too many patrons. His politics suited no one but himself. Younger muralists, including José Clemente Orozco and David Alfaro Siqueiros, continued to climb the scaffold. But Rivera split his time between politics, mainly applying to be readmitted to the Mexican Communist Party, and easel painting. His easel work sold well and was always in demand. He needed the money to support Frida; her sister, Cristina, and her children; Lupe and their two daughters; and Marika, his daughter by Marevna; as well as his two homes, San Angel and Casa Azul. As Hamill notes:

> He became the painter of the Indian, the artist who burned into the world's consciousness the image of the indigenous people of Mexico. . . . Rivera made the subject his own. In many oil paintings, hundreds of watercolors, and perhaps thousands of pencil and ink drawings he evoked the dignity, honor, and beauty of the Indians. Rivera painted numerous enduring works with Indian subjects, many of which are still being reproduced in posters and calendars decades after he made them.

Again and again Diego returned to the same themes: a pigtailed woman selling calla lilies, regional folk dancers, crowded marketplaces, men cutting sugar cane or carving wood, women making tortillas or caring for children, and the beautiful, brown-skinned children themselves in native dress.

Diego Rivera had become the artist of all Mexico, its regions, its history, and its people.

8

The Art of Frida Kahlo

Inasmuch as Rivera had become the artist of all Mexico, Frida Kahlo was also honing her own creative vision, securing her place among the nation's most admired painters. Kahlo's art channeled a range of emotions and ideas—from pain, love, and longing to explorations of identity, social politics, or nature. She possessed a unique beauty—it has been suggested that her connected eyebrows and faint mustache added to her allure. The majority of her approximately 200 paintings were self-portraits. In the course of her career, she drew on Mexican artistic traditions including religious ex-voto paintings to the darkly humorist engravings of José Guadalupe Posada, as well as Aztec and Christian imagery. Though she never considered herself a surrealist, the symbolic imagery she used in some of her works was reminiscent of surrealist techniques. Her paintings were typically small, in many cases no more than 12 by 15 inches. But her legacy

Frida Kahlo often inserted herself into her works. Her self-portraits sometimes included animals, with which she surrounded herself perhaps because she could not bear children.

is enormous. The mark she left on popular culture eclipsed that of her older husband.

Kahlo's artwork can be found on T-shirts, calendars, and other objects. In 2001, the U.S. Postal Service even issued a stamp in her honor. The following year, a major motion picture covered her life story and featured Salma Hayek in its starring role. "There is no artist in Mexico that can compare with her," Rivera once said of his wife. Not surprisingly, her work continues to endure today.

Kahlo's work is affecting, in part, because of its personal nature. In interviews, Kahlo said she painted in response to her own experience. "I paint my own reality," Kahlo once explained. "The only thing I know is that I paint because I need to, and I paint whatever passes through my head without any other consideration."

Her most famous pieces include her *Self-Portrait with Monkey*, which she created after her first one-woman exhibition in New York for the president of the city's Museum of Modern Art. Animals sometimes made appearances in her work; some critics suggest this was a product of both the loneliness and desire for children she experienced over her years with Rivera. Her *Self-Portrait on the Borderline Between Mexico and the United States*, meanwhile, juxtaposes images emblematic of Mexico's natural environment and ancient heritage against colder, mechanical images of industrial America. Spanning nearly 30 years, Kahlo's body of work came to be more widely appreciated decades after her death.

Early on, Kahlo embraced a muralistic style evident in her 1929 painting *The Bus*, which she finished during her fledgling romance with her future husband. Like Rivera's work, *The Bus* is inspired by a sense of social consciousness: The six characters depicted sitting inside the vehicle represent different social categories of wealth and influence. They include a heavyset woman with a straw shopping basket; a worker in blue denim overalls; a barefoot Indian mother with her infant; a young boy looking out the window; a white man in a suit holding what appears to be a bag of money; and a young, well-to-do Mexican woman. Kahlo's depictions point to disparities in wealth in Mexican society, while the painting's humorous

Kahlo spent time in the United States with Rivera, but she did not take a liking to the country. In San Francisco, she frequently was commissioned to paint portraits of society ladies *(above)*.

elements are, as Kahlo biographer Herrera points out, "pure Frida."

But where Rivera's early influence on Kahlo may have been seen in her artistic style, the couple's relationship also provided fodder for paintings conveying Frida's pain and sorrow. She was devastated that she was physically unable to bear Rivera's child. Shortly after their wedding, Frida had an abortion three months into her pregnancy (the fetus was in the wrong position). Several years later, she lost a child after two months of pregnancy and wound up spending 13 days in the hospital. This experience inspired a painting considered to be one of her best: *Henry Ford Hospital*. The piece is dark and unsettling, depicting Frida on a floating, bloody hospital bed holding ribbons connected to six objects: a fetus, two spinal columns, a snail, a piece of machinery, and a female torso. Rivera loved it, commenting that "Frida began work on a series of masterpieces which had no precedent in the history of art—paintings which exalted the feminine qualities of endurance, of truth, reality, cruelty, and suffering."

It was around this time that Frida finished *My Birth*, another dark piece that depicts Kahlo's mother giving birth to Frida. The mother appears corpselike, her face, chest, and arms covered with a white sheet. The child emerging from the woman's body, meanwhile, is disproportionately large. Kahlo's lithograph *Frida and the Abortion* also reflects a theme of conception, depicting a woman in various stages of pregnancy. Tears roll from her eyes and blood drips from her womb to fertilize a garden. Kahlo would have at least two abortions and a miscarriage in the course of her life; in her writing she expressed sorrow over having "lost three children." "Paintings substituted for all this," Frida once wrote. "I believe that work is the best thing."

Rivera's infidelity was also likely inspiration for Kahlo's art. Some have suggested *A Few Small Nips*, her gory depiction of a woman who'd been stabbed to death, was Kahlo's response to Rivera's 1934 affair with her sister Cristina. *The*

Wounded Table, which Kahlo painted shortly after her 1939 divorce, likewise, has been interpreted as a commentary on her situation with Rivera. It's a twist on the famous Leonardo da Vinci painting *The Last Supper*, placing Kahlo in the spot at the center of the table traditionally occupied by Christ. Other guests at the dinner table include Cristina's two children, a skeleton, a pre-Columbian sculpture, her pet fawn, and a papier-mâché Judas figure believed to represent Rivera. Intended to be burned as effigies during the Lenten season, such Judas figures were a Mexican tradition.

Herrera points out that the paintings Kahlo did of her and Rivera reflect various states of their marriage. The "wedding portrait" she finished in 1931, for example, was the first of several works demonstrating her deep affection and need for her husband; she depicts the couple holding hands. *The Love Embrace of the Universe* shows Rivera as a big baby, situated snugly on Kahlo's lap.

The couple's bond was fragile—Frida's *Diego and Frida 1929–1944* features the artist and her husband as a single head divided vertically into two halves. Their shared neck is adorned with a tree trunk with sharp, spiky branches. Inscribed on the frame are their names and the years they

THE TWO FRIDAS

Kahlo's divorce was the likely inspiration for one of Kahlo's largest and most famous works, *The Two Fridas*. It's a double self-portrait, showing two Kahlos sitting side-by-side. One has a visibly intact heart and the other a heart that has been damaged. The injured Frida holds a pair of surgical pincers, perhaps representative of her wish to cut off emotional ties to Rivera. The Frida with the intact heart, meanwhile, holds a portrait of Rivera attached to a vein suggesting an umbilical cord. "Diego's egg-shaped portrait thus seems to stand for both a lost baby and a lost lover," Herrera suggests. "To Frida, Diego was both."

were married. *Self-Portrait as a Tehuana*, meanwhile, includes an image of Diego resting atop Frida's eyebrows, showing that "Diego was a constant intruder in her thoughts," according to Herrera. Frida's 1949 painting *Diego and I* contains similar imagery. In her diary, Kahlo once asked, "Why do I call him My Diego? He never was nor ever will be mine. He belongs to himself."

Through the media, Kahlo and Rivera lived a public marriage, "the couple's every adventure, their loves, battles and separations . . . described in colorful detail by an avid press," says Herrera. The strain caused by Kahlo's marriage informed her art, as did her life-changing injury and illness, her cultural heritage and political beliefs. She is admired for celebrating what others might consider physical imperfections and for confronting adversity with strength and humor. To quote the Mexican writer Carlos Fuentes, "She is a figure that represents the conquest of adversity, that represents how—against hell and high water—a person is able to make their life and reinvent themselves and make that life be personally fulfilling. . . . Frida Kahlo in that sense is a symbol of hope, of power, of empowerment, for a variety of sectors of our population who are undergoing adverse conditions." She was, like Diego Rivera, a people's painter.

Final Touches

While Rivera concentrated on painting Indian themes and portraits of the rich and famous, he also renewed his interest in politics. He attended political functions and requested that Mexican President Lázaro Cárdenas grant political asylum to Leon Trotsky, who had been exiled from the Soviet Union by Stalin.

The best president since the revolution, Cárdenas had forced Plutarco Elias Calles, his corrupt predecessor known as "el Jefe Máximo de la Revolución," into exile in the United States. Cárdenas had restored the right of Catholic priests to say Mass in church. (That right had been taken away by Calles and led to the Cristero Rebellion.) He nationalized the foreign oil companies in Mexico. Taking the side of the poor, he distributed millions of acres of land to them, thus keeping the revolutionary promises of Emiliano Zapata.

Censorship plagued Rivera to the end of his life. His mural in Hotel del Prado was criticized for including the words, "God does not exist," which was pulled directly from a
speech delivered by the painting's subject, Ignacio Ramírez.

But Mexicans who supported Stalin did not like Cárdenas;
their dislike turned to hatred when he agreed to Diego Rivera's
request and allowed Trotsky to enter the country. Of course,
they had detested Rivera for some time. Rivera had been an
anti-Stalinist since his expulsion from Moscow, where he was
denied a wall to paint.

As guests of the Riveras, Trotsky and his wife lived in Casa Azul for two years. Fearing Stalinist assassins, the Trotskys turned Casa Azul into a fortress by barricading doors, filling windows with adobe bricks, and surrounding themselves with armed guards. Casa Azul was the site of a Joint Commission of Inquiry in the Moscow Trials. Chaired by the philosopher John Dewey, the Dewey Commission, as it was also called, cleared Trotsky of Stalin's accusations against him. In the United States, Dewey was criticized for his participation. Trotsky was elated by the findings, although they led to Stalin's intensified persecution of Trotskyists worldwide.

Trotsky did not participate in Communist activities in Mexico, but he did write, expressing his views about art and revolution in magazine articles. And he had an affair with Frida, who soon tired of the gray-haired man with the goatee, whom she called "El Viejo," the Old Man. She may have started the brief affair as a payback to Diego for his affair with her sister. Although she and Diego apparently never discussed her affair, they divorced in 1939 after she returned from her six-month trip to New York and Paris to exhibit her paintings for the first time.

Trotsky and Rivera admired each other. The Russian called Rivera's frescoes magnificent interpretations of the October Revolution. Trotsky said that his words could convince a few people at a time that socialism was best, while Diego's art could convince hundreds all at once. Rivera preferred Trotsky's politics to Stalin's. But their relationship became strained after Rivera found out about Trotsky's affair with Frida.

Trotsky and his wife moved to another villa not far from Casa Azul, which they also made into a fortress. Two years later, David Alfaro Siqueiros—a muralist, a former revolutionary fighter, and a Stalinist—led an assassination attempt on Trotsky. He and several other gunmen fired 173 machine-gun bullets into the bedroom of the fortified villa where the Trotskys were living, but they failed to hit either Trotsky or his wife, who hid under the bed. Siqueiros was jailed for a year before being exiled to Chile.

RIVERA'S ESCAPE TO THE UNITED STATES

Because Rivera had received several death threats, he went into hiding and left the country. He accepted a commission to paint a 10-panel mural on movable steel frames on Treasure Island in San Francisco Bay as part of the Golden Gate International Exposition. The theme was *Pan-American*

RENAISSANCE MEN

The "Mexican Mural Renaissance" of the 1920s and 1930s is typically credited to three artists: Diego Rivera, José Clemente Orozco, and David Alfaro Siqueiros. Each studied at the San Carlos Academy for Fine Arts and experimented with the classical tradition of fresco painting. Each spent time working in the United States. And each created enduring pieces that reflected postrevolutionary Mexican politics and put art in the public domain, accessible to all people regardless of social class. Though these men are often discussed in the same breath, it's important to note that Rivera, Orozco, and Siqueiros each possessed a distinct artistic style and political outlook.

Orozco's work often reflected a theme of human struggle. Unlike Rivera, he was a pessimist and had little faith in organized political movements. His interest in art began 1890, when, as a young boy, he passed by the open workshop of the master Mexican engraver José Guadalupe Posada. Though he initially planned to work as an architect, a gunpowder accident that eventually resulted in the loss of his left hand helped ensure that this wouldn't happen. Determined to become a serious painter, he entered the academy at San Carlos in 1905, when he was in his early 20's.

Orozco's pessimism was driven by life experience. He began his career amid the 10-year civil war that raged throughout Mexico after the 1910 revolution. He resided in

Unity. As he painted high on his scaffold in an airplane hangar being used as an exhibition hall during the summer of 1940, he had an audience. Below him, thousands of people walked past and watched the artist at work. He enjoyed entertaining the crowds.

REMARRIAGE TO FRIDA

In August of 1940, a single assassin, Ramón Mercader, drove a mountaineer's ice pick into Trotsky's head. Because Frida had

the United States during the Great Depression in the early 1930s. Visiting Europe briefly in 1932, he was exposed to the rise of fascism. Where Rivera's paintings embodied a more realistic approach, Orozco was more of an expressionist—that is, he distorted imagery to convey emotion. Orozco believed that painting "assails the mind" and "persuades the heart." Today, he is one of Mexico's most revered artists, and his murals can be seen in various schools and public buildings in the U.S. and Mexico.

David Alfaro Siqueiros was a Stalinist whose art often depicted ordinary people struggling against oppression. Deeply influenced by his political beliefs, his work is often described as "social realism." Stylistically, he was known for his swirling brushstrokes, brilliant colors, and incorporation of new tools and techniques, including airbrushes. He created or collaborated on a number of murals, including those at the National Preparatory School in Mexico City, the Mexican Electrical Workers Union building, National Institute of Fine Arts, and the Hotel de Mexico. His politics extended beyond his art—he once served as a leader of the Syndicate of Technical Workers, Artists, and Sculptors and helped found *Machete*, its magazine, which promoted public art. He was active in the Mexican Communist Party, as well, but was expelled in 1932 and again in 1940 for his role in the attempted assassination of Leon Trotsky.

met the handsome Spanish assassin in Paris, she was suspected of being an accomplice. Police interrogated her for 12 hours, and they ransacked Rivera's house. When Diego heard of the rough treatment of Frida, he arranged for her to join him in San Francisco. She did, and, after a two-year separation, the couple remarried on December 8, 1940, Diego's 54th birthday.

The couple returned to Mexico after Diego completed the mural in San Francisco. Rivera applied for, and was denied, readmission to the Mexican Communist Party. He would apply five times before finally being readmitted; Frida's readmission occurred before his.

During the next few years, Diego and Frida both suffered from ill health. They had several operations and were in a great deal of pain. But both artists continued to paint. Marnham explains, "[Frida's] art grew through their relationship and was partly the consequence of it. She was, as she herself said, painting her private reality. But Rivera was trying to paint abstract ideas; his art was independent of their relationship, formed by earlier experience."

In 1943, Rivera was invited to his first teaching post since he was pushed to resign from the San Carlos Art Academy in 1930. It was at the Education Ministry's Academy of Painting and Sculpture in Mexico City, where he would teach alongside another new faculty member and fellow national treasure, his wife Frida Kahlo—until Frida's health forced her to transfer classes to the Blue House. Frida's pupils became known as "Los Fridos"; Diego's were "los Dieguitos." One former student, Arturo García Bustos, contrasted the two instructors' teaching styles. Frida "never said a word about how we were supposed to paint or questions of style, as we were accustomed to hearing from Diego Rivera," he said. Another, Fanny Rabel, told writers Isabel Alcántra and Sandra Egnolff that Rivera could "develop a theory from absolutely anything in no time at all; the *maestra*, on the other hand, was intuitive and spontaneous."

One year after their divorce, Kahlo and Rivera remarried. Their union would continue until Kahlo's death.

FOCUS ON PAINTING THE PAST

Early in his life, Rivera had painted the future. One example was the final panel in the stairway of the National Palace. Late in his life, he looked increasingly to the past. His most striking fresco in the corridor of the same palace, done in the 1940s, is his dream of the past, the Aztec capital of Tenochtitlán before the Spanish Conquest.

In his personal life, also, Rivera dreamed of the past. He designed and built a monumental stone house similar in shape to a pyramid, which would be a studio for his easel painting, a museum for his vast collection of Aztec stone idols and other ancient artifacts, his retirement home, and eventually, he thought, his tomb. He applied what remained of his waning energy to the building of this strange edifice at Anahuacalli on the lava bed of a long-dead volcano, the Pedregal, barren except for cacti and other drought-resistant flora that thrive in the harsh landscape. Inspired by the Great Temple of Tenochtitlán, the structure was built of irregularly cut stone taken from the ancient lava flow itself.

Diego spared no expense in its construction, spending an enormous amount of money on both the building and the artifacts he displayed inside. The pyramid in Anahuacalli, its collection of artifacts, and Casa Azul were Diego's gifts to the people of Mexico after Frida's death.

DECLINING YEARS

Toward the end, Diego often glanced back over his life, even as he lived in the present. He wrote:

> One of my greatest excitements now is seeing my newest grandson, Ruth's baby. Ruth calls him Zopito, meaning "Little Frog," because he is fat like me, whom she calls Zoporana, "Big Frog." It's funny that people I love most think I look like a frog, because the city of Guanajuato where I was born means "Many Singing Frogs in Water." I am certainly not a singing frog, though I do burst forth on rare happy occasions into a song.

Some of the art Rivera painted in his declining years shows that his creative powers were not at their peak. *The Nightmare of War and the Dream of Peace*, done in 1952, is considered his worst mural. The Mexican government had commissioned it, but when officials saw his depiction of Stalin and Mao Tse-tung as heroes, they turned it down. Rivera returned his fee. He sent the mural, which had been done on movable panels, to the People's Republic of China, where it disappeared.

He applied again and again for readmission to the Communist Party, but his requests were denied. While Frida was alive, he spent time in his studio in San Angel (preferring to work there when doing portraits), in his pyramid in Anahuacalli (sorting and displaying his stone idols), and in Casa Azul (Frida's home).

"Rivera could be very nice or very difficult," recalled Ella Wolfe, the wife of Bertram Wolfe. Diego was always nice when the Wolfes visited Casa Azul, a lively household, where monkeys jumped through the window during lunch, snatched food off the table, and ran off to eat it. Seven hairless Xólotl dogs lived in the Blue House, too. When one of them urinated on a just-completed Rivera watercolor, Diego grabbed a machete and chased the little dog until he cornered it. Cowering against the wall, the dog seemed to be begging for mercy. Diego picked it up, lowered his weapon, and told the dog, "Lord Xólotl, you are the best art critic I know."

Rivera never lost his power to charm, and he was especially good at charming women. Although he looked like a frog and did not bathe often, women were attracted to his hypnotic personality because he flattered them, treating them as though they mattered to him. But, by his own admission, he could be cruel to women he loved, especially Frida.

Rivera also never lost his ability as a storyteller. Listeners were fascinated by his narrative fantasies. Guadalupe, his older daughter by Lupe Marín, said that her father fictionalized the events of his life, changing the story daily. Listeners enjoyed hearing him tell his tale, and they knew it was fiction. Marnham elaborates on Rivera's love of storytelling:

> In the last decade of his life Rivera took increasing pleasure in his skills as a storyteller. He devoted his inventive power to

his autobiography, reliving his life as a fable, rather as he had relived the Aztec past as a fable in the National Palace. *My Art, My Life* is the biographical equivalent of the magical realism school of fiction.

And it is the most riveting account of the actual and legendary life of Diego Rivera and well worth the time it takes to read the short book, which the artist "dictated" to writer Gladys March during several interviews while he painted in his studio. March calls the work "Rivera's apologia: a self-portrait of a complex and controversial personality, and a key

REMEMBERING PAPA

When she was just a little girl, Guadalupe Rivera Marín posed with an orange for her father, the painter Diego Rivera. During the session, she apparently got a bit hungry. Before her father completed his final brushstrokes, young Guadalupe had begun eating the fruit. "I was so young at the time and didn't realize what it meant to pose for him," admits Marín, quoted in an Aug. 13, 2009, article about her then-forthcoming book in *Publishers Weekly*. "I never knew my father was such a great painter. He was just my father. Finally, when I was a teenager, I began to understand how important he was and I started to understand him and to be interested in how he created art."

In September 2009, Children's Book Press was scheduled to publish Marín's work, a picture book containing both her recollections of life with her dad and commentary on 13 of his works of art (including the one in which she posed with the orange). Marín's goal is to help people better understand her father's personal side and, especially, his love of children. "He paid so much attention to children in his work, Mexican children especially, because he found that they were the future of the country," she told *Publishers Weekly*.

to the work of perhaps the greatest artist the Americas have yet produced."

AUTOBIOGRAPHY IN ART

Rivera's last great fresco (started in 1942), another of his dreams of the past, was a pictorial autobiography. Commissioned for the restaurant of Hotel del Prado, which faced one side of Alameda Park in Mexico City, the mural was painted on portable frames 50 feet long by 16 feet high. Rivera outdid himself in the large space, crowding more than 150 figures from his own and his country's past into the mural. He himself appears to the left of center as a fat youth with bulging, froglike eyes. Wearing a straw hat, short pants, and striped socks, he holds an umbrella adorned with a vulture's head in one hand. A frog peeks out of one jacket pocket; a snake crawls out of another. Behind him stands an adult Frida Kahlo, who rests her hand on his shoulder as though to protect him. "Beside the boy is an image of death wearing a boa hat, a grinning skeletal version of la calvera Catrina as depicted by José Guadalupe Posada [the Mexican engraver whom Diego claimed had been his teacher]. Death gently holds the boy's hand; her other hand is on the arm of a bowler-hatted Posada."

The mural is Diego Rivera's nostalgic, yet humorous, view of Mexican society and its cast of historical characters, both heroes and villains, from the time of the Spanish Conquest to the revolution of 1910. This autobiographical work, called *Dream of a Sunday Afternoon in Alameda Park*, is truly a masterpiece. But it was defaced, repainted, and then censored for nine years (hotel owners covered it with a white nylon screen) because of one small artistic detail that aroused the ire of Catholics. On the far left side of the mural, Rivera painted the words from an 1836 speech delivered by Ignacio Ramírez, *El Nigromante*: "Dios no existe," or "God does not exist." Rivera refused to change the words, saying they were not his. He had been raised Catholic, but he called himself an atheist for most

DIEGO RIVERA'S LEGACY

DIEGO RIVERA'S LEGACY

Throughout his career as an artist, Rivera had a tenuous relationship with his beloved Mexico. Though he wanted to please his countrymen with art that was available to the common public, his controversial political beliefs and unusual sense of humor often set him at odds with his country. At his death, however, Mexico ultimately recognized Diego Rivera as one of its greatest citizens. As Gladys March writes in the introduction to Rivera's autobiography, *My Art, My Life*, Rivera was honored with a hero's burial:

> Dressed in a blue suit and tie and a red shirt, and sheathed in a casket of brown steel, the remains of Diego Rivera were lowered into the earth of the Rotunda of Mexico's Illustrious Men, Dolores Cemetery. In the same hallowed ground lie the bones of Benito Juárez, Mexico's greatest hero.

of his life. Diego had risen from a sickbed to paint it. When he finished, he kept painting, despite poor health. Frida's health worsened, too.

ILLNESS BESETS FRIDA AND DIEGO

In April 1953, Frida Kahlo's paintings were exhibited in a one-woman show at the Galería de Arte Contemporáneo in Mexico City. She was brought to the opening in an ambulance and taken on a stretcher to a four-poster bed in the gallery. Many people attended, paying tribute to what Diego called her great talent. A few months later, Frida's right leg was amputated below the knee. Afterward, she seemed to lose her will to live and sank into depression. She wrote a suicide note in her diary and died in 1954 at the age of 47, possibly of an overdose of painkillers. Earlier, she'd presented Rivera a ring for their silver wedding anniversary more than a month early. "I feel I am going to leave you very soon," she told him. Diego called the July day on which she died the most tragic of his life.

Funeral services were held in the Palacio de Bellas Artes. Diego assured the museum's director, a friend of his named Andrés Iduarte, that he would not turn the ceremony into a Communist event. But he refused to remove a red flag decorated with a gold hammer and sickle, the flag of the Communist Party, that had been draped over his wife's coffin. Iduarte lost his job because of the display, and Rivera was finally readmitted to the Communist Party after his fifth application in September 1953. In his autobiography, he noted this was his "only comfort" in the wake of Frida's death. Rivera was so upset after the ceremony at the crematorium, by one account, that he swallowed a handful of Frida's ashes.

For whatever anguish he may have caused her, Rivera held his wife's art in the highest regard. He has been quoted as having referred to Frida as the "most important Mexican artist" and suggested her body of work "represents one of the most powerful and truthful human documents of our times." A year after her death, he honored her with a drawing that included the following dedication: "For the star of my eyes, Fridita, who is still mine, 13 July 1955, Diego. It was a year ago today."

His mourning didn't prevent Rivera from marrying his fourth wife, his art dealer Emma Hurtado, just 16 days after the one-year anniversary of Frida's death. Hurtado was at Rivera's side when he traveled to Moscow in pursuit of treatment for his prostate cancer. When he returned to Mexico, he claimed that "the cobalt bomb" had cured him. It had not.

In April 1956, Diego Rivera made final touches to his public art for what would be the last time. He painted over Ignacio Ramírez's words "Dios no existe" on the mural at the Hotel del Prado and replaced them with "Lecture at the Letrán Academy, 1836," which was the date and place of the Ramírez's speech. Two days later, he held a press conference and announced,

Diego Rivera lived life to the fullest. Although he is most known for his passion and his volatile relationship with Frida Kahlo, his true legacy is as Mexico's premiere muralist, one who influenced generations of artists to create public art that displayed social conscience.

"Soy Católico!" (I am a Catholic!). He explained his action by saying, "I admire the Virgin of Guadalupe. It is my desire to gratify my countrymen, the Mexican Catholics, who comprise 96 percent of the population of the country."

On November 24, 1957, the *pintor magnífico* died in his San Angel studio. His instructions that his ashes be mingled with Frida Kahlo's, which were kept at Casa Azul, were not followed. He would be interred (buried) in a location befitting his stature. He was important to the people of Mexico, whom he had loved. For them he had burst forth into song on the happy occasions when he painted their story in his larger-than-life murals.

Chronology

1886
Diego María Rivera born on December 8 in Guanajuato, Mexico

1905
Awarded scholarship to study art in Europe

1913
Begins painting in the cubist manner

1922
Marries Guadalupe Marín. Joins Mexican Communist Party

1886   1929

1898
Enters the national school of art, the San Carlos Academy of Fine Arts

1920
Receives grant from Mexican government to tour Italy and study fresco paintings of Renaissance masters

1929
Marries Frida Kahlo

1916   In New York, exhibit of his paintings with those of Cézanne, van Gogh, Picasso, and Braque. A son named Diego is born to Angeline, but he lives only 14 months.

1917   Breaks with cubist painters. October Revolution in Russia.

1919   Daughter Marika born to his lover, Marevna Vorobev.

1920   Earns money by painting portraits. Receives grant from Mexican government to tour Italy and study fresco paintings of Renaissance masters.

1921   Returns to homeland alone at invitation of Mexican government to paint murals on walls of public buildings.

1922   Marries Guadalupe Marín. Joins Mexican Communist Party. With several artists starts Union of Technical Workers, Painters and Sculptors. Begins first mural, *Creation*.

1931 — 1957

1932
Works on *Detroit Industry*, commissioned by the Detroit Institute of Arts in Michigan

1947
Begins last fresco, *Dream of a Sunday Afternoon in the Alameda*

1957
Dies on November 24

1954
Kahlo dies after long illness

1931
Paints two major frescoes in the United States

1937
Persuades Mexico's president to grant refuge to Russian revolutionary Leon Trotsky

1933
Begins *Man at the Crossroads* fresco Rockefeller Center

1955
Marries art dealer Emma Hurtado

1923 Begins series of murals in the Ministry of Education.

1924 Daughter Guadalupe born to Guadalupe Marín. Begins mural at the chapel of the University of Chapingo.

1927 Daughter Ruth born to Guadalupe Marín. Travels to Soviet Union for anniversary of October Revolution after separating from wife.

1929 Not allowed to paint fresco in Moscow. Expelled from Soviet Union. In Mexico, begins murals at the National Palace. Marries Frida Kahlo.

1931 Paints two major frescoes in the United States at the Pacific Stock Exchange and at San Francisco Art Institute. Returns to work on frescoes at National Palace in Mexico. One-man show at New York's Museum of Modern Art.

1932 Works on *Detroit Industry*, commissioned by the Detroit Institute of Arts in Michigan.

1933 Detroit fresco inaugurated despite controversy. Begins *Man at the Crossroads* fresco in RCA Building lobby in Rockefeller Center. Fresco viewed as Communist propaganda and work stopped after Rivera refuses to remove portrait of Lenin. Completes *Portrait of America* at New York's New Workers School before return to Mexico.

1934 *Man at the Crossroads* destroyed at Rockefeller Center. Begins reproduction, *Man, Controller of the Universe*, in Mexico City.

1936 Paints *Burlesque of Mexican Folklore and Politics* for Hotel Reforma. Portable panels never installed because of controversial subject.

1937 Persuades Mexico's president to grant refuge to Russian revolutionary Leon Trotsky.

1940 Unsuccessful assassination attempt on Trotsky by Siqueiros. Rivera paints mural for Golden Gate International Exposition in San Francisco. Trotsky assassinated in Mexico.

1942   Begins fresco in corridor of National Palace.

1947   Begins last great (autobiographical) fresco, *Dream of a Sunday Afternoon in the Alameda*.

1948   Alameda fresco covered by a curtain and hidden from public view after his refusal to remove the words "Dios no existe!" ("God does not exist!").

1954   Kahlo dies after long illness.

1955   Marries art dealer Emma Hurtado, who accompanies him to Moscow for cancer treatment.

1956   Paints over the words, "Dios no existe!" on the Alameda fresco. Announces, "I am a Catholic." National celebrations honor his 70th birthday.

1957   Dies on November 24. Buried in the Rotunda of Mexico's Illustrious Men in Mexico City.

Bibliography

Alcántara, Isabel and Sandra Egnolff. *Frida Kahlo and Diego Rivera*. New York: Prestel (Pegasus Library), 1999.

Hamill, Pete. *Diego Rivera*. New York: Harry N. Abrams, Inc., 1999.

Hein, Hilde S. *Public Art: Thinking Museums Differently*. Lanham, Md.: AltaMira Press, 2006.

Herrera, Hayden. *Frida: A Biography of Frida Kahlo*. New York: Harper Perennial, 2002.

Herrera, Hayden. "Jose Clemente Orozco and Diego Rivera: The Murals." Unpublished lecture delivered November 16, 1990, Metropolitan Museum of Art, New York. Mary-Anne Martin/Fine Art. Available online. URL: http://www.mamfa.com/exh/oroz1996/hh_article.htm.

Lee, Anthony W. *Painting on the Left: Diego Rivera, Radical Politics and San Francisco's Public Murals*. Berkeley: University of California Press, 1999.

Lodge, Sally. "Diego Rivera's Daughter Shares Memories of Her Father." *Publishers Weekly*. Available online. URL: http://www.publishersweekly.com/article/CA6676470.html. Updated on August 13, 2009/13/2009.

Marnham, Patrick. *Dreaming With His Eyes Open: A Life of Diego Rivera*. Los Angeles: University of California Press, 1998.

Morrison, John F. *Frida Kahlo*. New York: Chelsea House Publishers, 2003.

Pomade, Rita. "From a Mexican Perspective— The Vision of Adolfo Best Maugard." MexConnect.com. Available online. URL: http://www.mexconnect.com/articles/1080-from-a-mexican-perspective-the-vision-of-adolfo-best-maugard. Updated on January 1, 2006.

Rivera, Diego (with Gladys March). *Diego Rivera: My Art, My Life, An Autobiography*. New York: Dover Publications, 1991.

Rochfort, Desmond. *Mexican Muralists, Orozco, Rivera, Siqueiros*. San Francisco: Chronicle Books, 1993.

Rochfort, Desmond. *The Murals of Diego Rivera*. London: Journeyman Press, 1987.

Wolfe, Bertram D. *The Fabulous Life of Diego Rivera*. New York: Stein and Day, 1963.

Further Reading

Arquin, Florence. *Diego Rivera: The Shaping of an Artist, 1889–1921.* Norman, Oklahoma: University of Oklahoma Press, 1971.

Hargrove, Jim. *Diego Rivera: Mexican Muralist.* Chicago: Children's Press, 1990.

Marín, Guadalupe Rivera. *My Papa Diego and Me/Mi papá Diego y yo.* San Francisco: Children's Book Press, 2009.

Rivera, Diego (with Gladys March). *Diego Rivera: My Art, My Life, An Autobiography.* New York: Dover Publications, 1991.

Rochfort, Desmond. *The Murals of Diego Rivera.* London: Journeyman Press, 1987.

Web Sites

Brain Juice, "Frida Kahlo"
http://www.brain-juice.com/

Cityclubsf.com
http://www.cityclubsf.com/new_art_and_arch.htm

Diego Rivera at the Detroit Institute of Arts
www.dia.org/art/rivera-court.aspx

The Life and Times of Frida Kahlo
http://www.pbs.org/weta/fridakahlo/

The Virtual Diego Rivera Web Museum
http://www.diegorivera.com/index.html

Artist Diego Rivera
http://www.pbs.org/newshour/bb/entertainment/july-dec99/rivera_7-15.html

The Diego Rivera Mural Project
http://www.riveramural.com

American Masters, Orozco: Man of Fire
http://www.pbs.org/wnet/americanmasters/episodes/jose-clemente-orozco/orozco-man-of-fire/82/

Picture Credits

Index

About the Author

Sheila Wood Foard earned a bachelor's degree and master's degree from the University of New Mexico. She taught journalism, writing, and literature at Del Norte High School in Albuquerque for 25 years. She has written profiles of New Mexicans and feature articles for the *Albuquerque Journal*. Her fiction, nonfiction, and poetry have appeared in various magazines for young readers.

Jamie Pietras is a writer and journalist who lives in New York City. He holds an M.F.A. in creative writing with a concentration in nonfiction from Columbia University.